DREAM·THEATER
METROPOLIS PT.2: **SCENES FROM A MEMORY**

About the Transcriptions:
These transcriptions were meticulously edited by John Petrucci in order to ensure the accuracy and playability of the notes and fingerings.

Transcribed by Danny Begelman and John Petrucci

Project Manager: Aaron Stang
Music Editor: Colgan Bryan
Technical Editor: Jack Allen
Engraver: Rosario Ortiz
CD Art Direction and Design: Lili Picou
Cover Illustration: Dave McKean
House Photography: Andrew Lepley
Still Life Photography: Ken Schles
Book Art Layout: Carmen Fortunato

WARNER BROS. PUBLICATIONS - THE GLOBAL LEADER IN PRINT
USA: 15800 NW 48th Avenue, Miami, FL 33014

WARNER/CHAPPELL MUSIC

NUOVA CARISCH

INTERNATIONAL MUSIC PUBLICATIONS LIMITED

CANADA: 15800 N.W. 48th AVENUE
MIAMI, FLORIDA 33014
SCANDINAVIA: P.O. BOX 533, VENDEVAGEN 85 B
S-182 15, DANDERYD, SWEDEN
AUSTRALIA: P.O. BOX 353
3 TALAVERA ROAD, NORTH RYDE N.S.W. 2113
ASIA: UNIT 901 - LIPPO SUN PLAZA
28 CANTON ROAD
TSIM SHA TSUI, KOWLOON, HONG KONG

ITALY: VIA CAMPANIA, 12
20098 S. GIULIANO MILANESE (MI)
ZONA INDUSTRIALE SESTO ULTERIANO
SPAIN: MAGALLANES, 25
28015 MADRID
FRANCE: CARISCH MUSICOM,
25, RUE D'HAUTEVILLE, 75010 PARIS

ENGLAND: GRIFFIN HOUSE,
161 HAMMERSMITH ROAD, LONDON W6 8BS
GERMANY: MARSTALLSTR. 8, D-80539 MUNCHEN
DENMARK: DANMUSIK, VOGNMAGERGADE 7
DK 1120 KOBENHAVNK

Contents

SCENE ONE: REGRESSION

Music and Lyrics by
JOHN PETRUCCI

0441B

SCENE TWO: I. OVERTURE 1928

Music by
DREAM THEATER

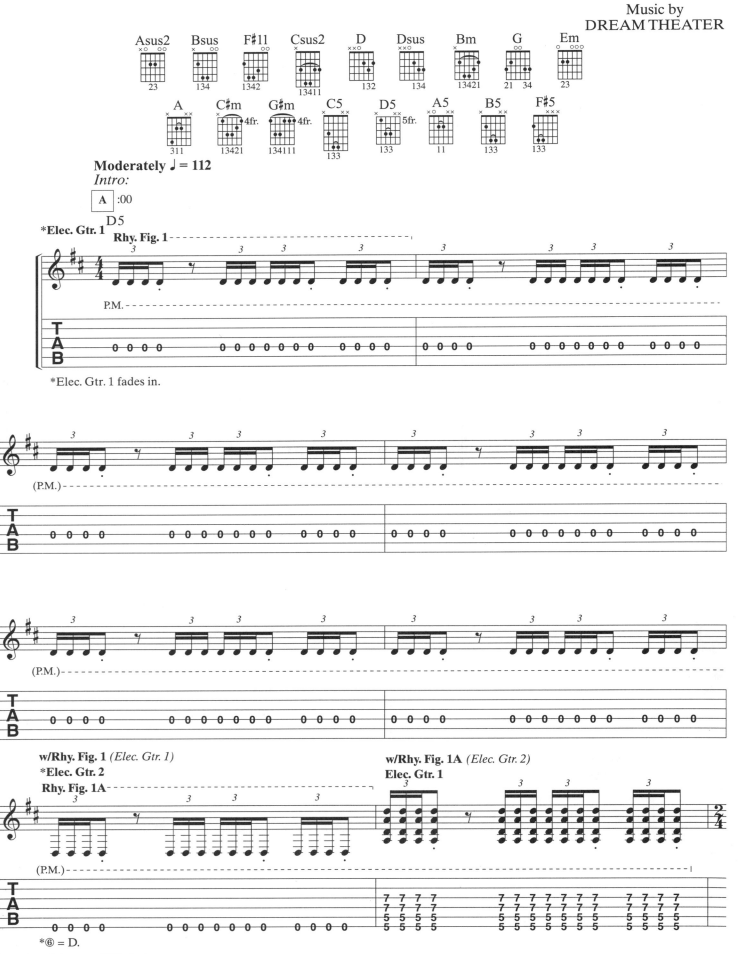

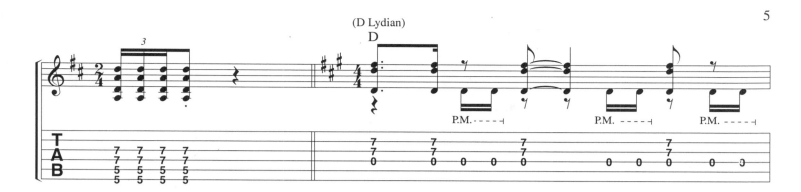

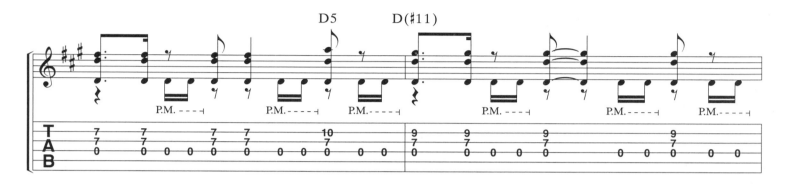

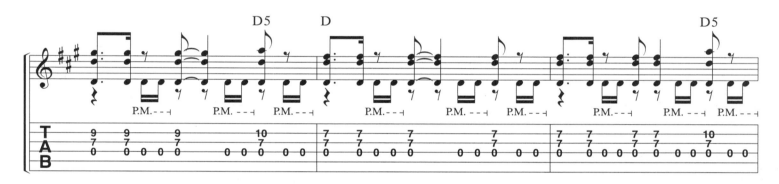

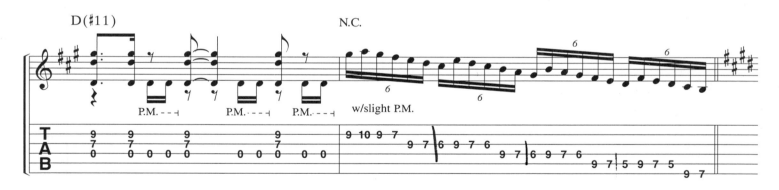

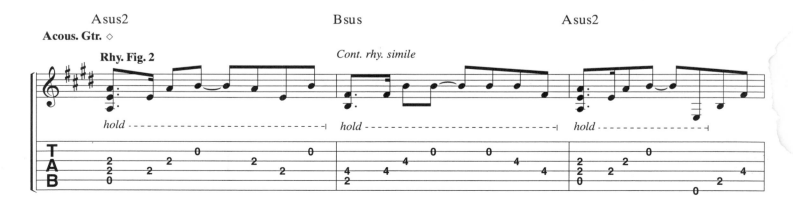

Scene Two: I. Overture 1928 - 8 - 2
0441B

5

6

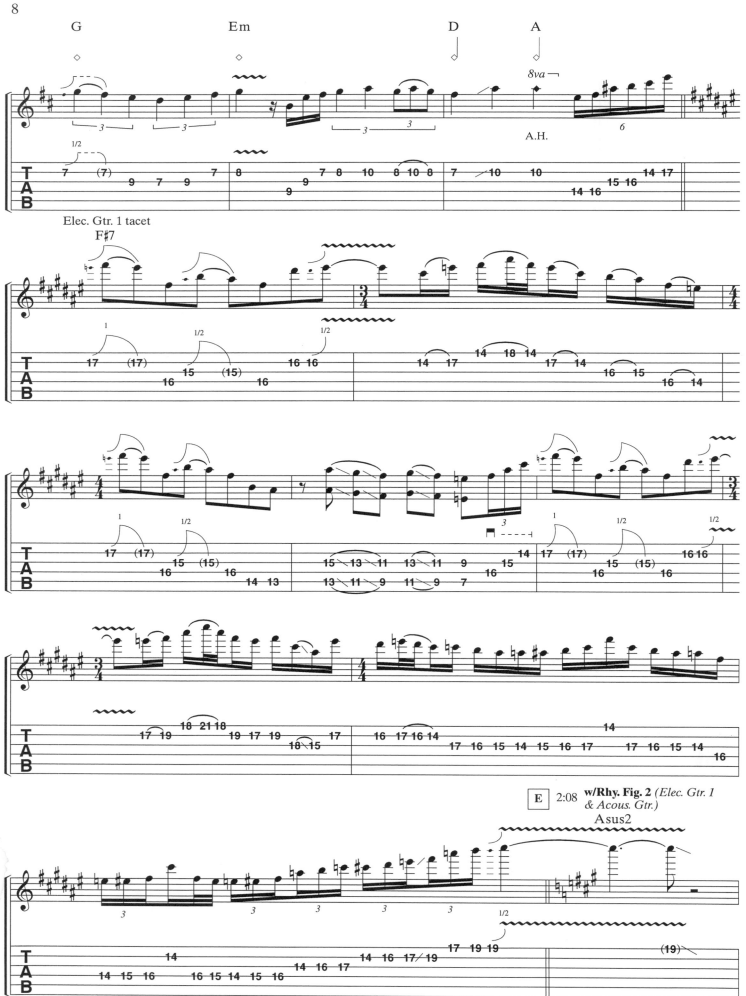

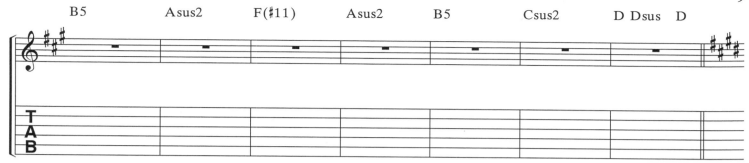

F 2:26

Guitar Solo 2:

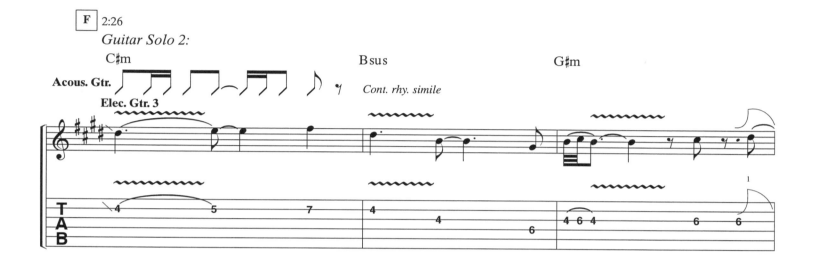

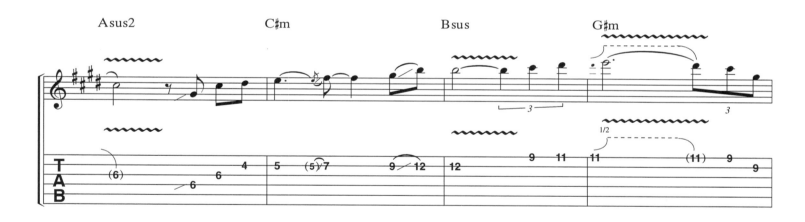

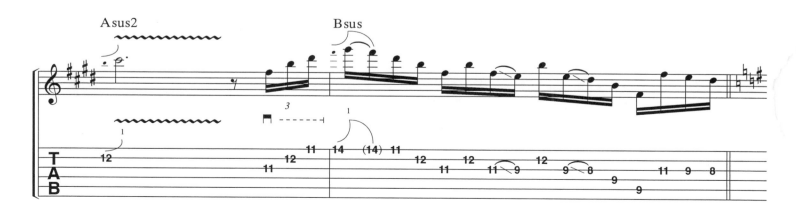

Scene Two: I. Overture 1928 - 8 - 6
0441B

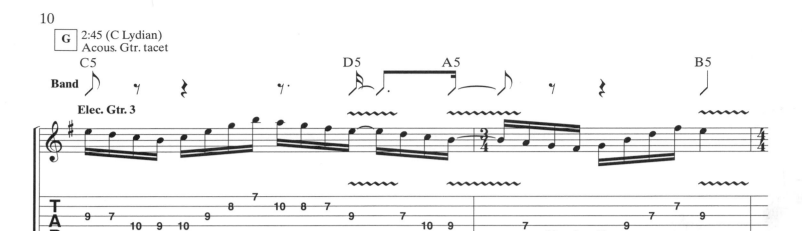

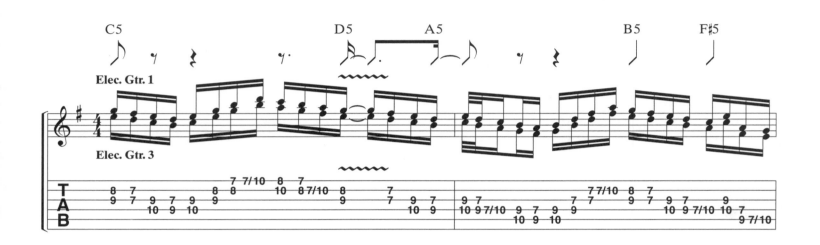

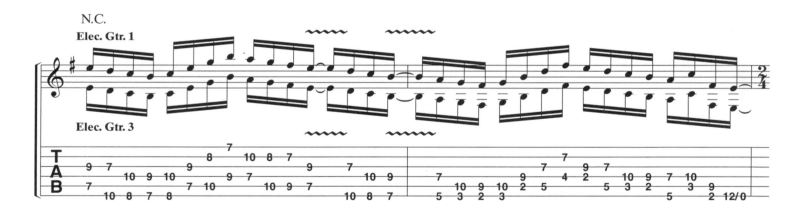

Scene Two: I. Overture 1928 - 8 - 7
0441B

SCENE TWO: II. STRANGE DÉJÀ VU

Music by DREAM THEATER
Lyrics by MIKE PORTNOY

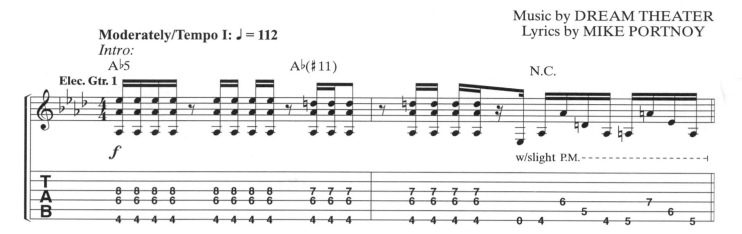

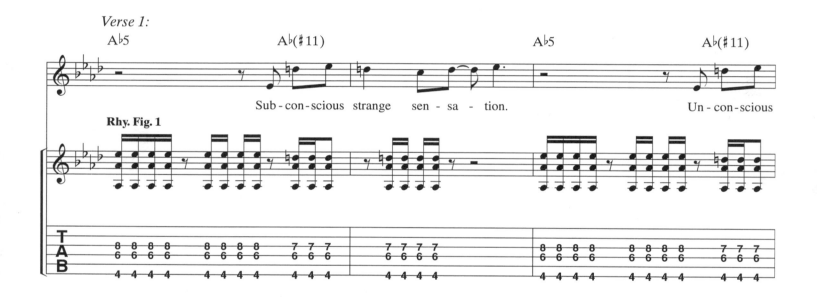

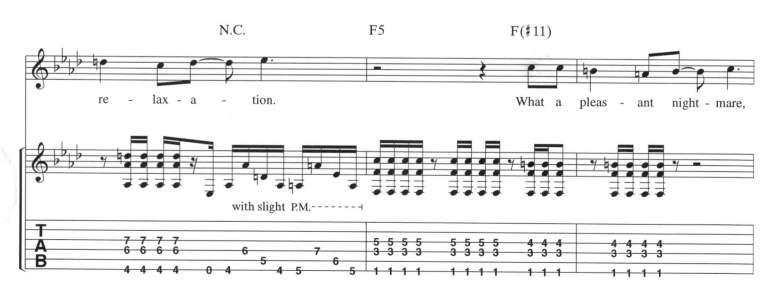

Scene Two: II. Strange Déjà Vu - 14 - 1
0441B

Verse 2:

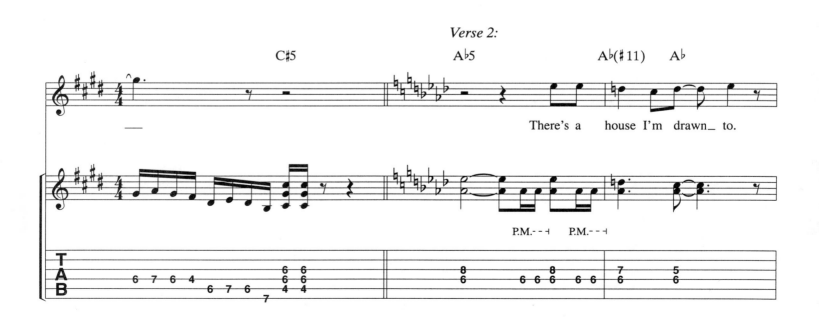

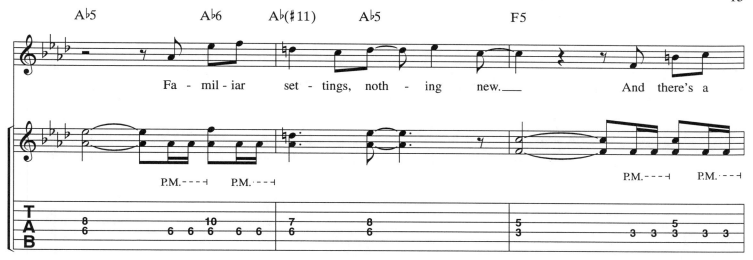

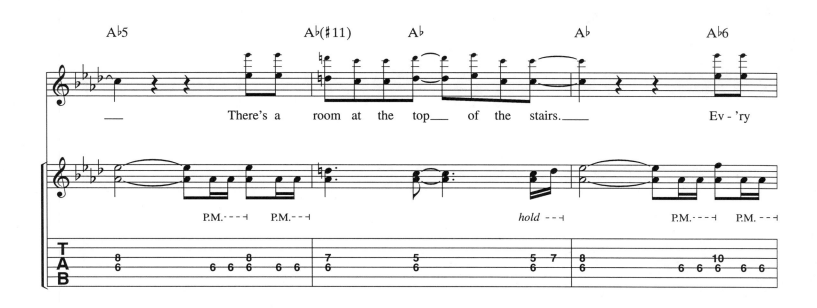

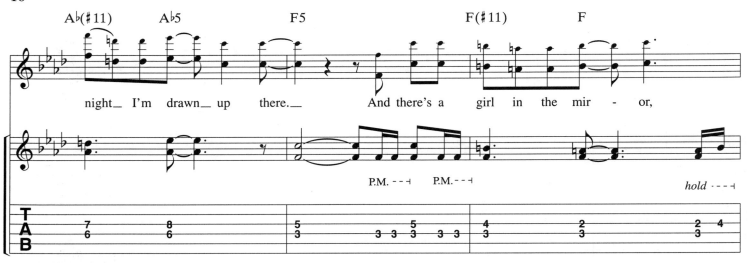

night_ I'm drawn_ up there.__ And there's a girl in the mir - or,

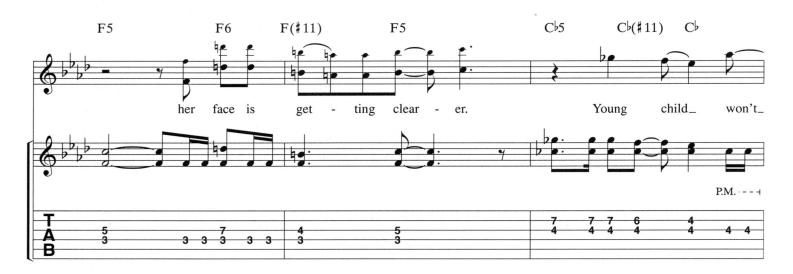

her face is get - ting clear - er. Young child_ won't_

__ you tell_ me why I'm_ here._____

w/**Riff A** *(Elec. Gtr. 1)*

In her____ eyes, I sense a sto - ry nev - er told.__

Be-hind the__ dis - guise,____ there's some-thing tear - ing at__ her soul.__

Pre-chorus 1:

To - night__ I've been search - ing for____ it,

Elec. Gtr. 1

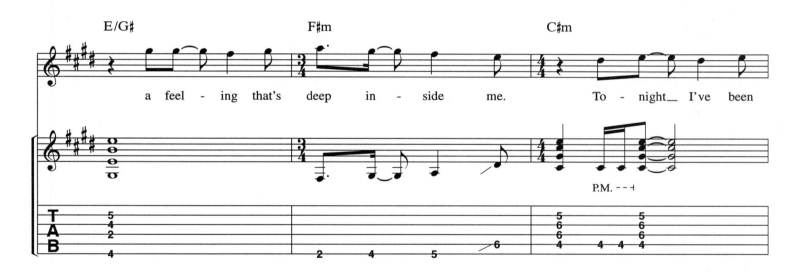

a feel - ing that's deep in - side me. To - night__ I've been

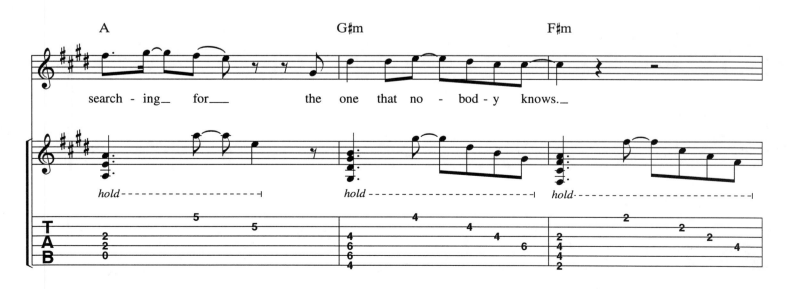

search - ing__ for___ the one that no - bod - y knows.__

hold-   hold-   hold- -

Chorus:

*Elec. Gtr. 1 dbld. by Acous. Gtr.

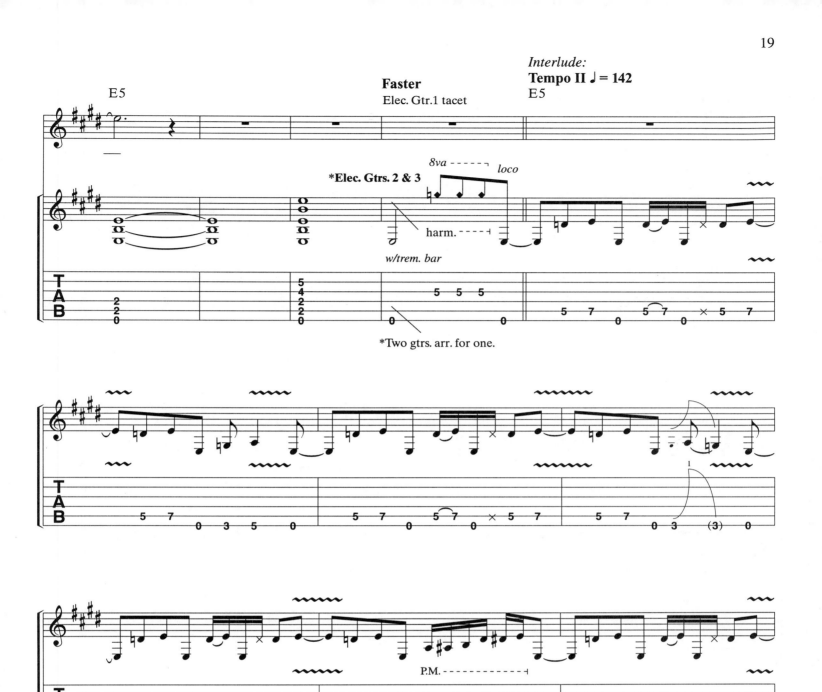

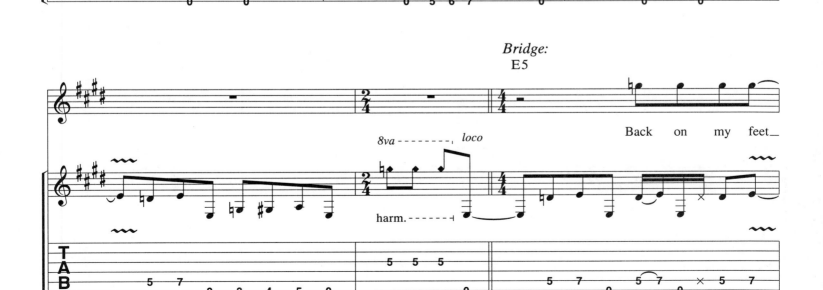

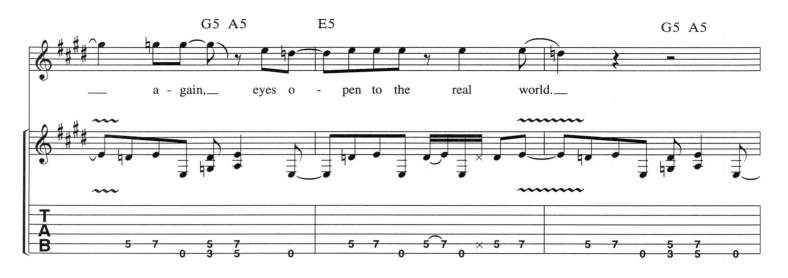

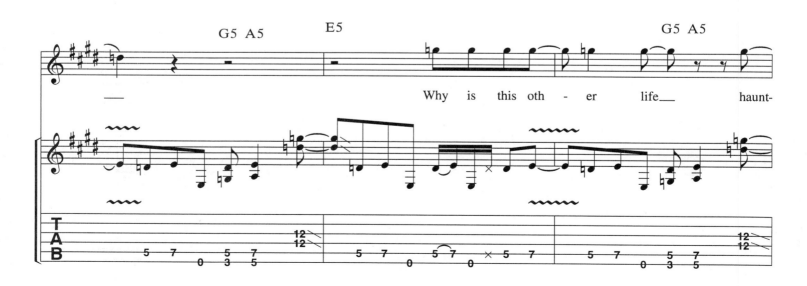

Some - thing's aw - f'lly fa - mil - iar, the feel - ing's so hard___ to shake.

Elec. Gtrs. 2 & 3

___ Could I have lived in that oth - er world,___ it's a

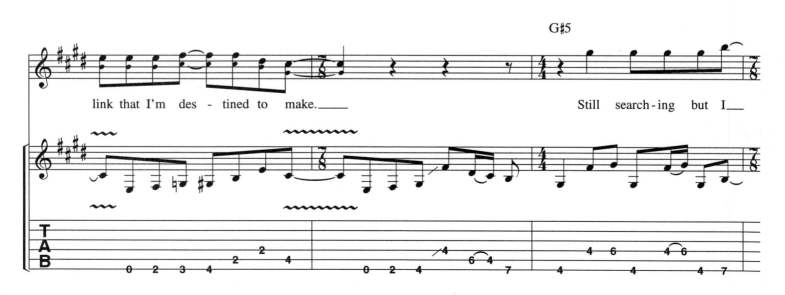

link that I'm des - tined to make._____ Still search - ing but I___

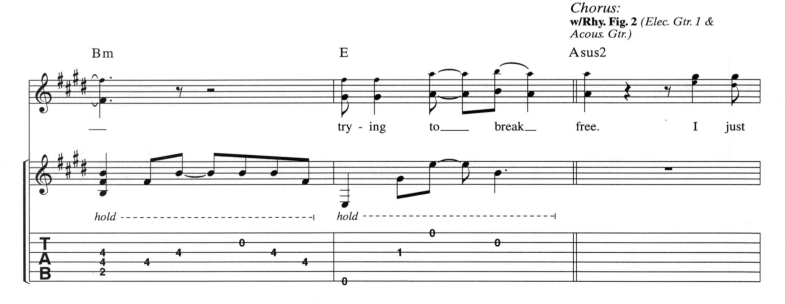

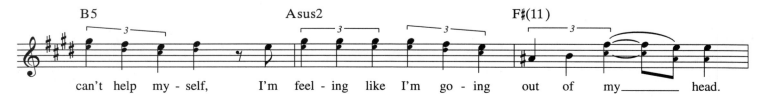

Scene Two: II. Strange Déjà Vu - 14 - 13
0441B

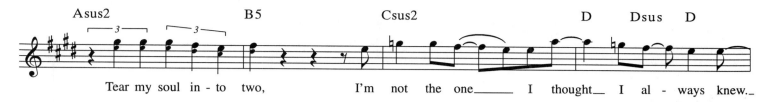

Tear my soul in-to two, I'm not the one___ I thought___ I al-ways knew.

w/Rhy. Fig. 2 *(Elec. Gtr. 1 & Acous. Gtr.) 1st 6 meas. only*

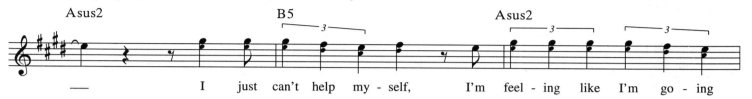

___ I just can't help my-self, I'm feel-ing like I'm go-ing

out of my___ head. Un-can-ny, strange dé-jà vu, but

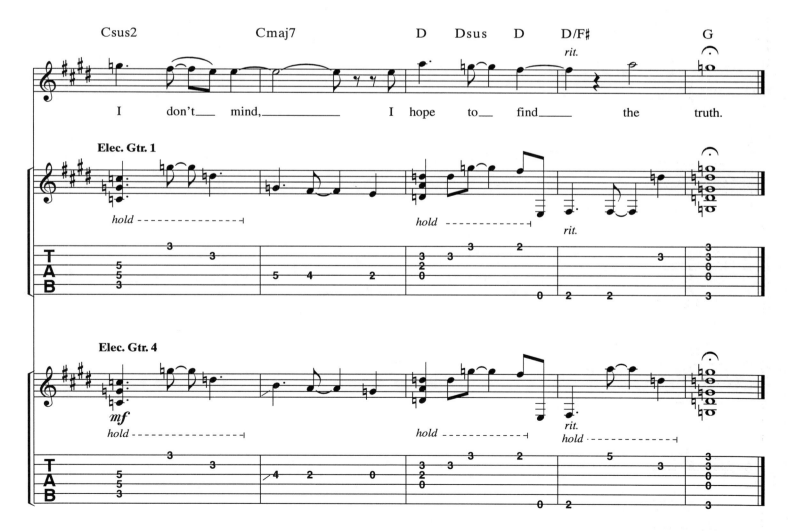

I don't___ mind,___ I hope to___ find___ the truth.

SCENE THREE: I. THROUGH MY WORDS

Music and Lyrics by
JOHN PETRUCCI

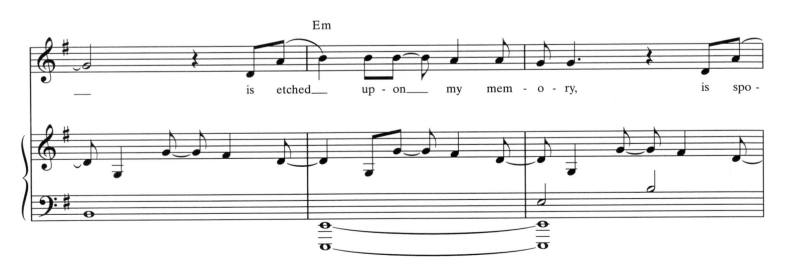

Scene Three: I. Through My Words - 3 - 1
0441B

D

Gmaj7

im - pos - si - ble___ to break.___

Segue to Fatal Tragedy

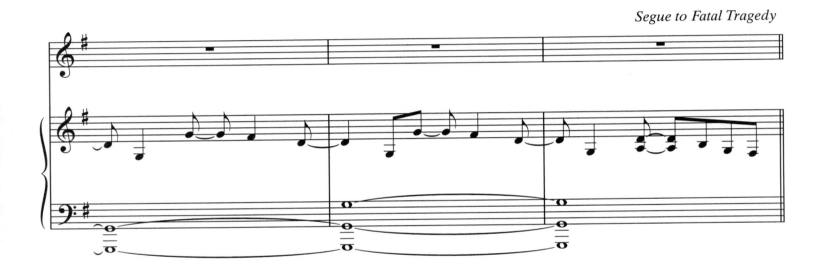

SCENE THREE: II. FATAL TRAGEDY

Music by DREAM THEATER
Lyrics by JOHN MYUNG

Segue from Through My Words

Slowly ♩ = 54

Scene Three: II. Fatal Tragedy - 18 - 1
0441B

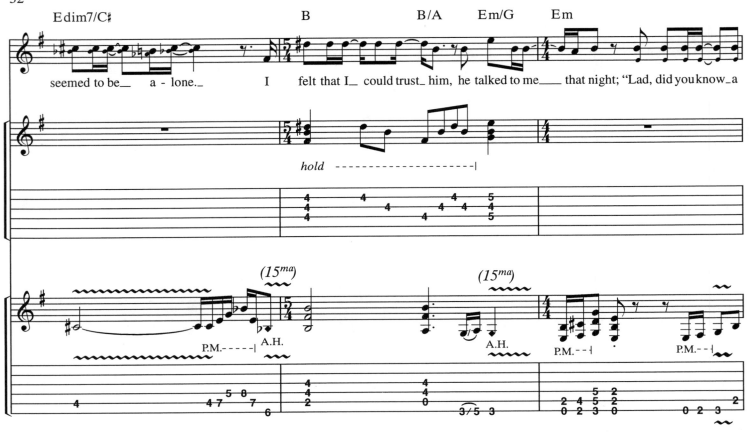

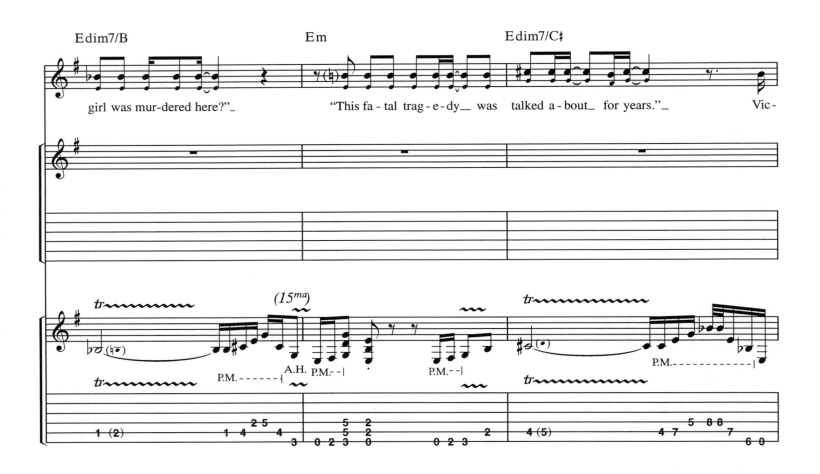

34

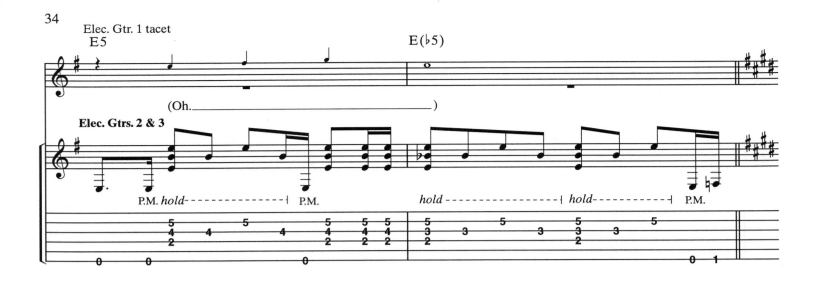

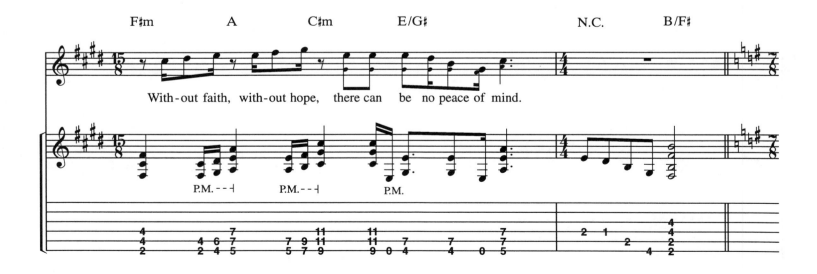

Elec. Gtrs. 4 & 5 tacet

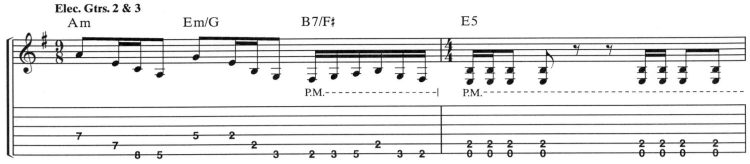

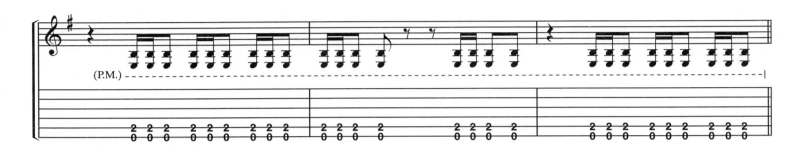

Verse 2:

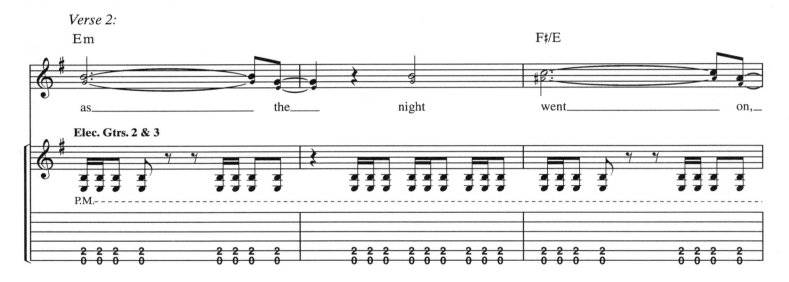

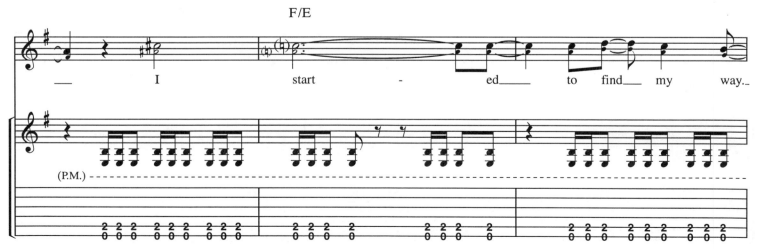

40

A 3:50 *Instrumental Section:*
Elec. Gtr. 2 Riff A
* Em

*Band enters on repeat.

end Riff A
Play 3 times

B 4:11

P.M.

P.M.

Scene Three: II. Fatal Tragedy - 18 - 13
0441B

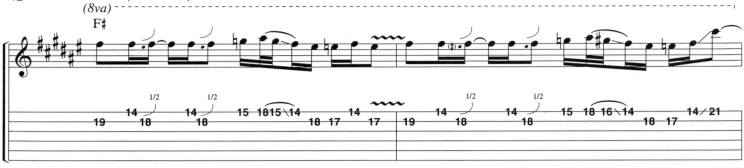

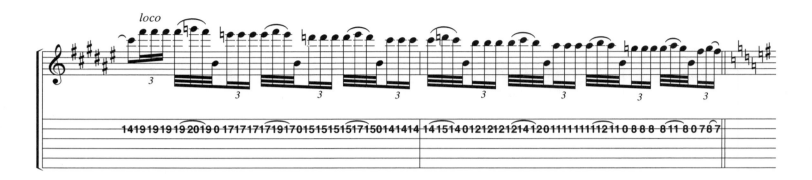

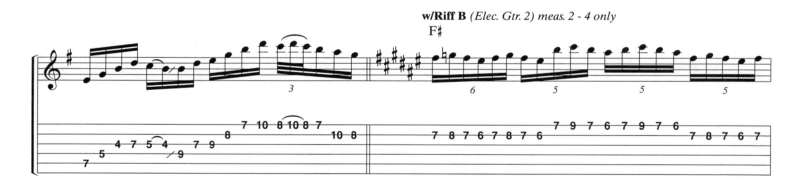

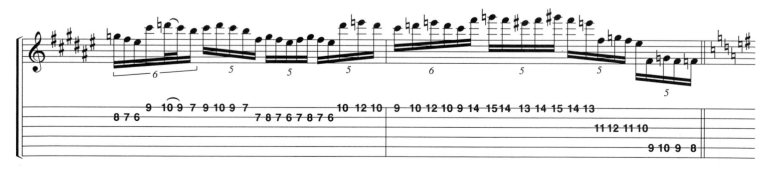

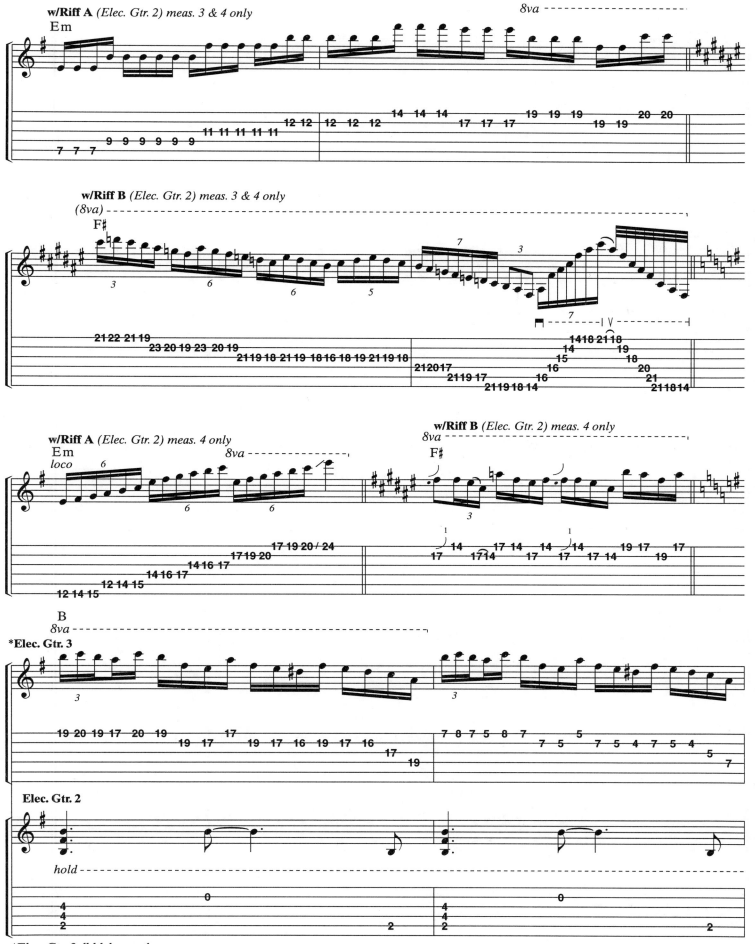

*Elec. Gtr. 3 dbld. by synth.
Scene Three: II. Fatal Tragedy - 18 - 15
0441B

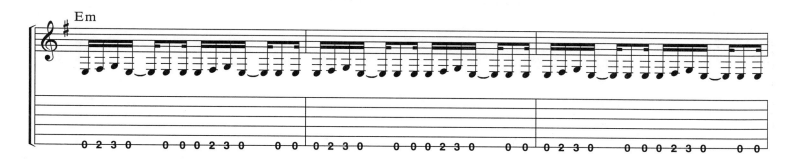

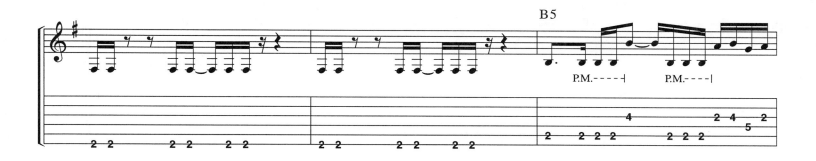

Scene Three: II. Fatal Tragedy - 18 - 17
0441B

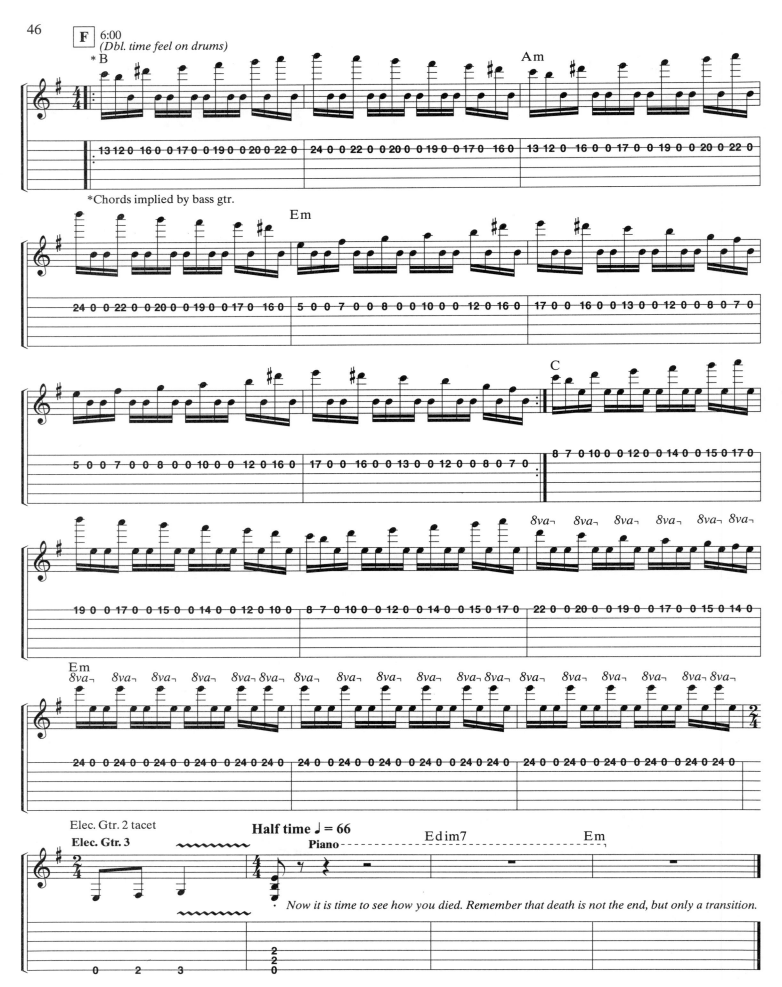

SCENE FOUR: BEYOND THIS LIFE

Music by DREAM THEATER
Lyrics by JOHN PETRUCCI

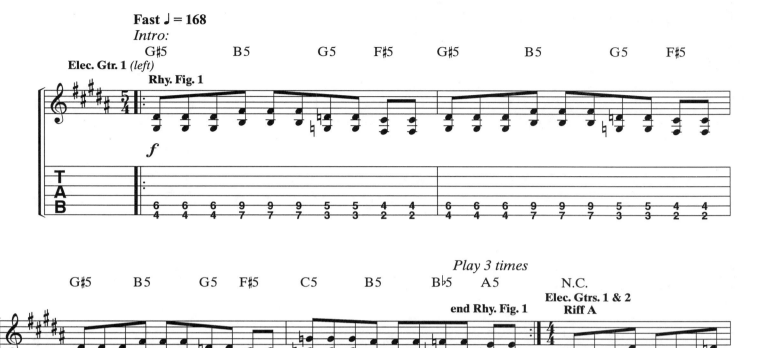

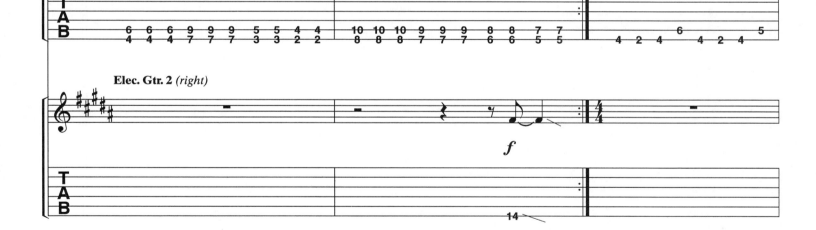

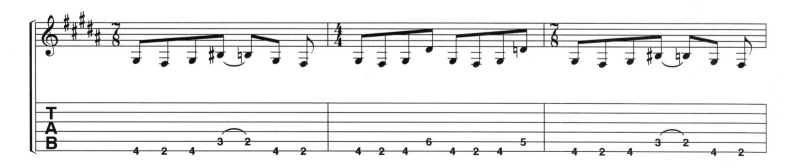

Scene Four: Beyond This Life - 33 - 1
0441B

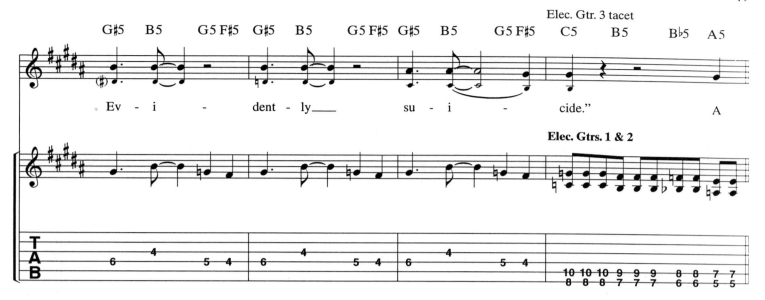

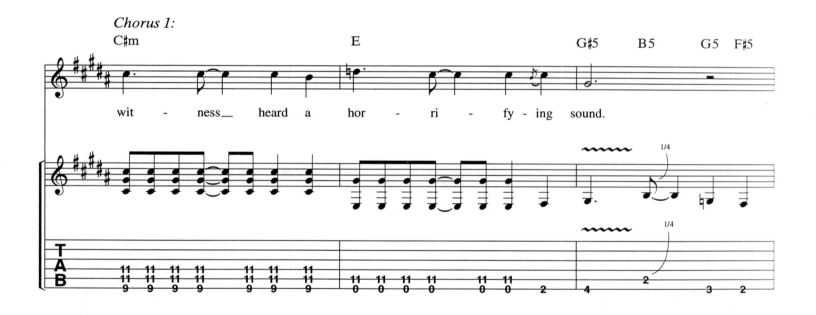

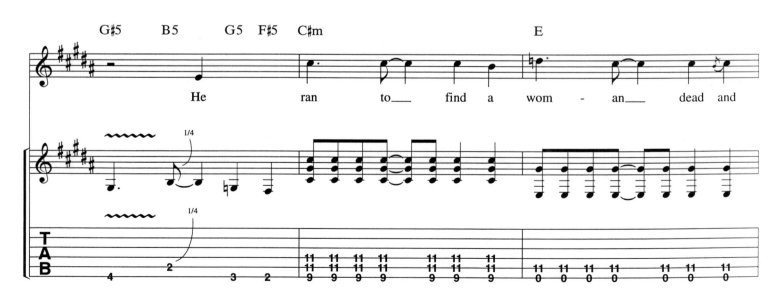

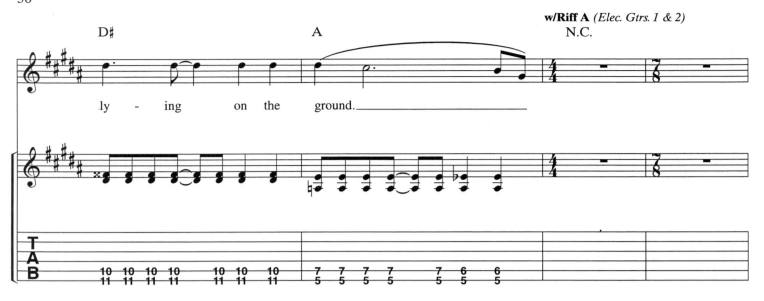

*Chords implied by bass gtr.

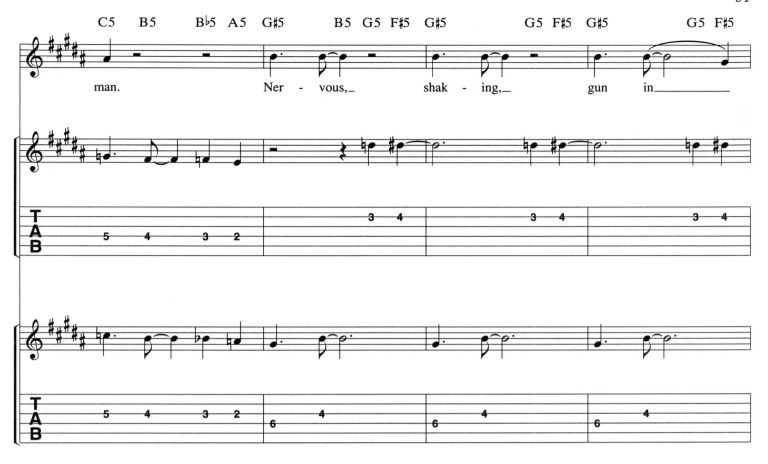

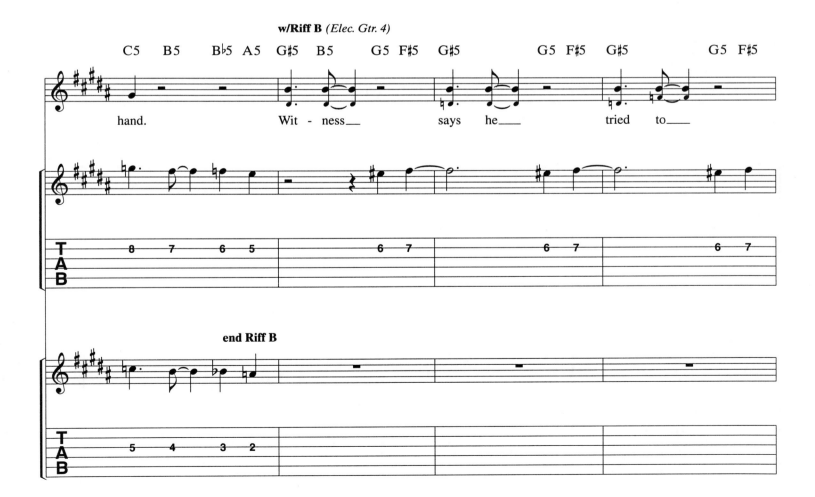

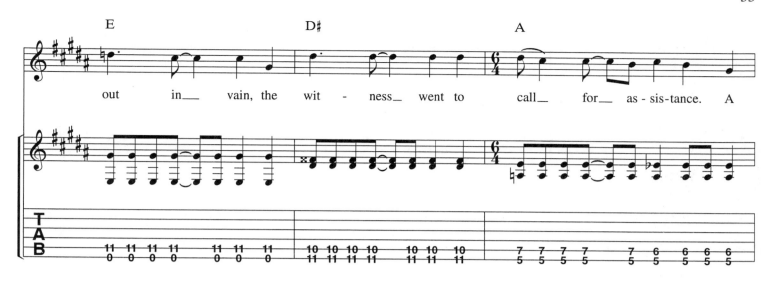

out in____ vain, the wit - ness____ went to call____ for____ as - sis-tance. A

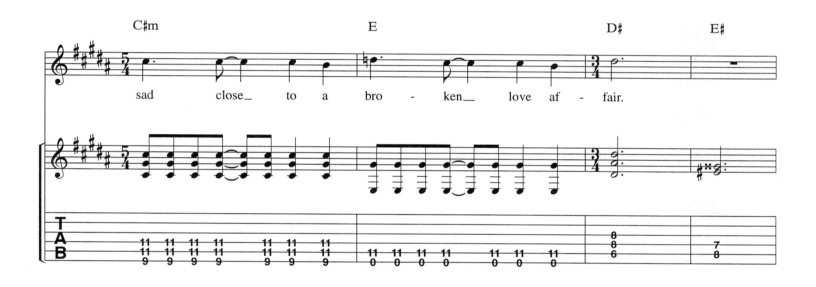

sad close____ to a bro - ken____ love af - fair.

Bridge 1:

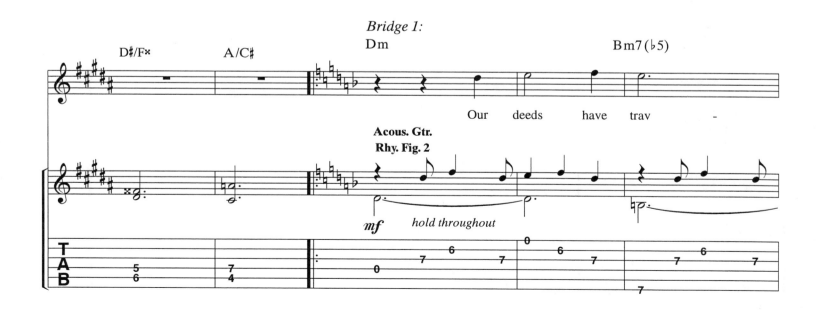

Our deeds have trav -

Acous. Gtr.
Rhy. Fig. 2

mf *hold throughout*

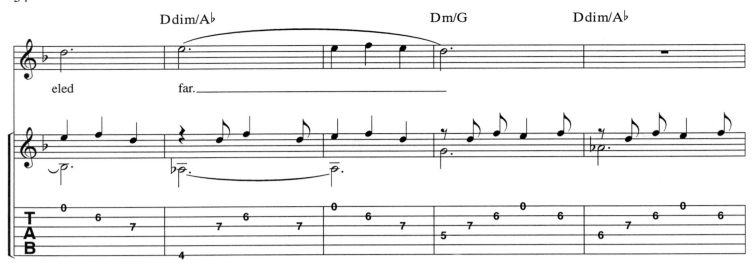

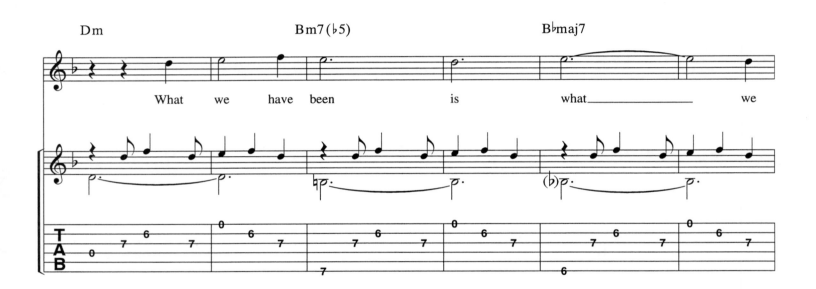

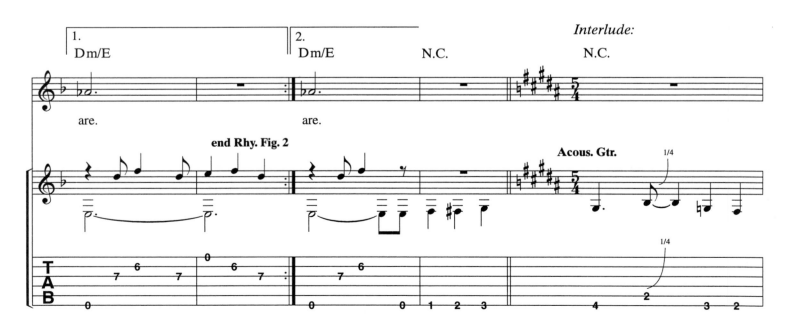

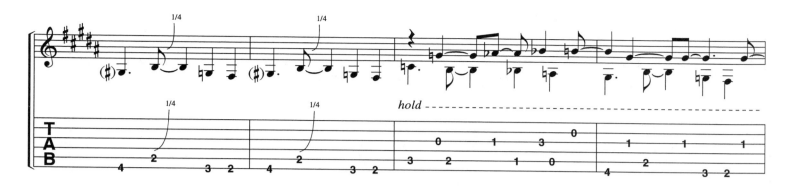

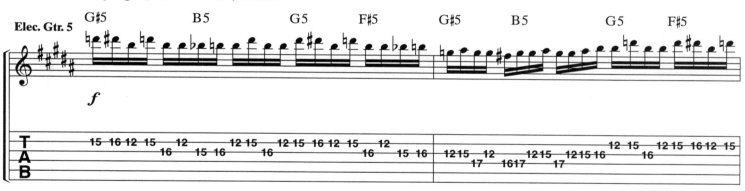

Guitar Solo:
w/Rhy. Fig. 1 *(Elec. Gtrs. 1 & 2) 2 times*

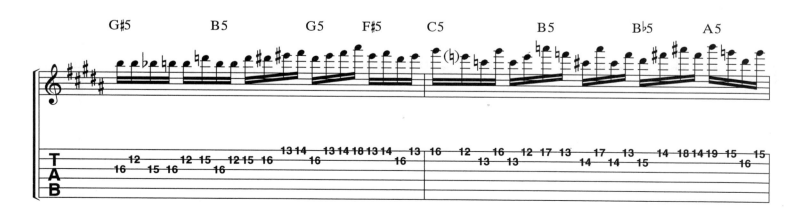

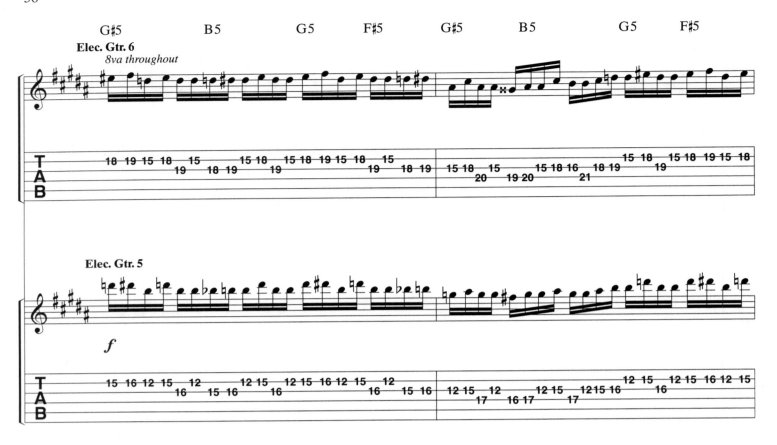

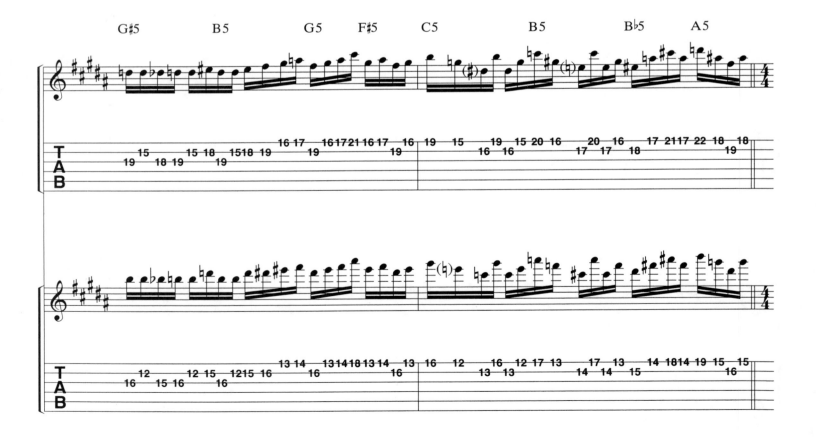

58

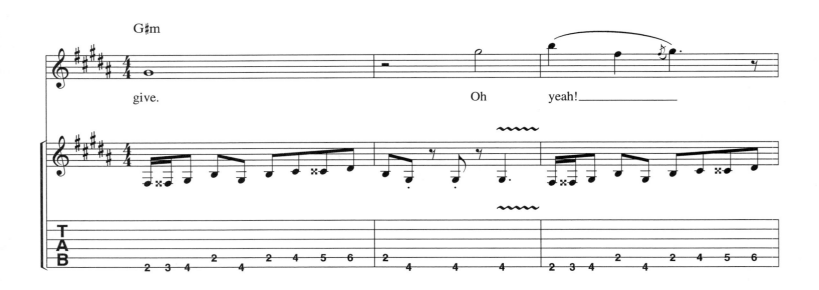

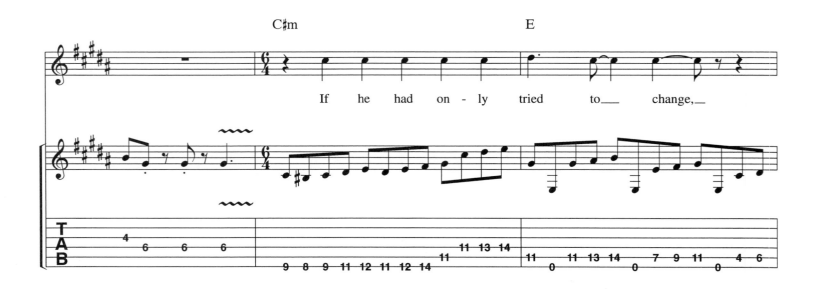

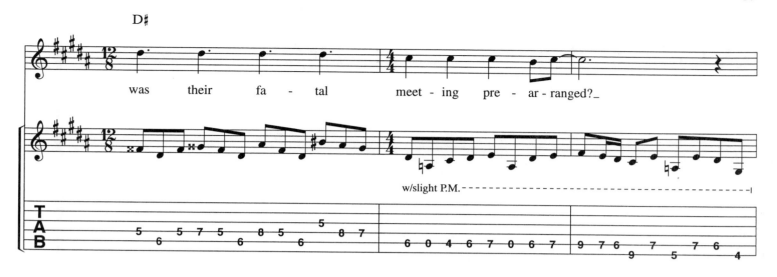

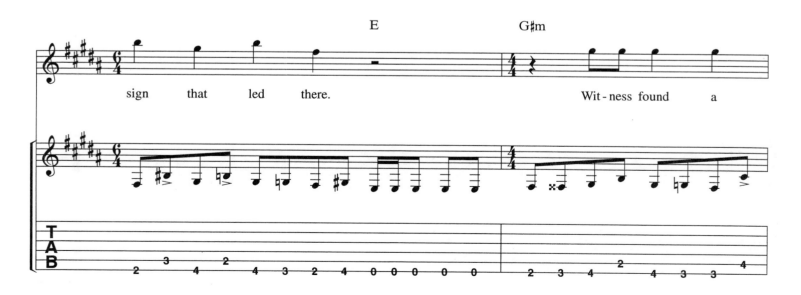

switch-blade   on the ground.   Was the vic - tim   un - a - ware?

w/Riff D *(Elec. Gtrs. 1 & 2)*

They con-tin-ued   to   in-ves-ti-gate.   They found a note in the   kill-er's pock-et.

It could have been a   su - i - cide let - ter.   May-be he had   lost her love.

N.C.
Elec. Gtrs. 1 & 2

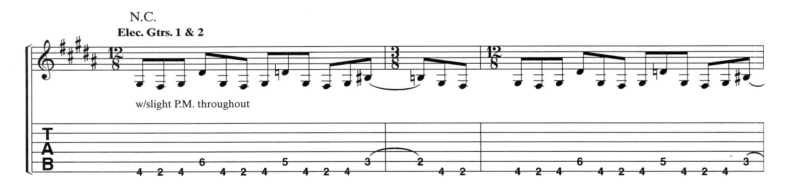

w/slight P.M. throughout

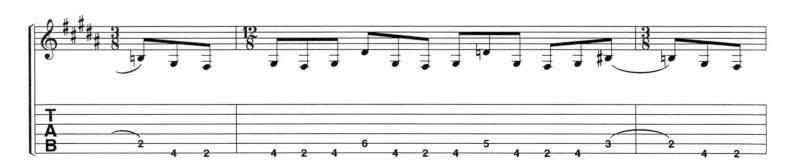

life a - way__ than live with los - ing you.

Bridge 2:
w/Rhy. Fig. 2 (*Acous. Gtr.*)

Our deeds have trav - eled far._____

*Elec. Gtrs. 1 & 2

**Elec. Gtr. 8

(End of Instrumental section)

*2nd time (𝄋) only.
**2nd time (𝄋) only.

What we have been is

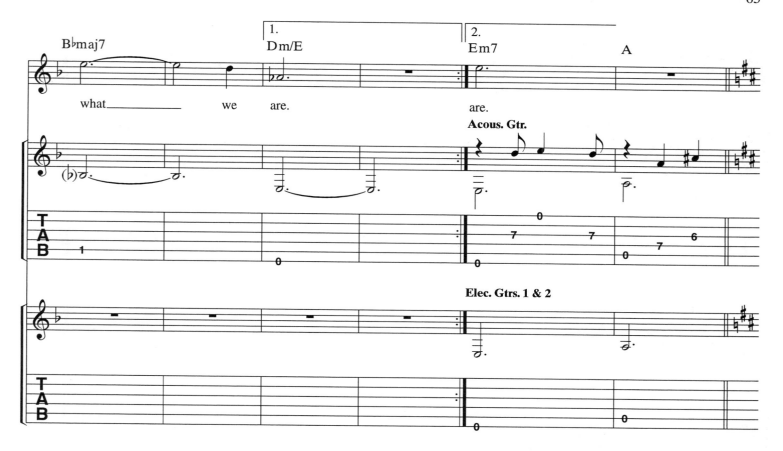

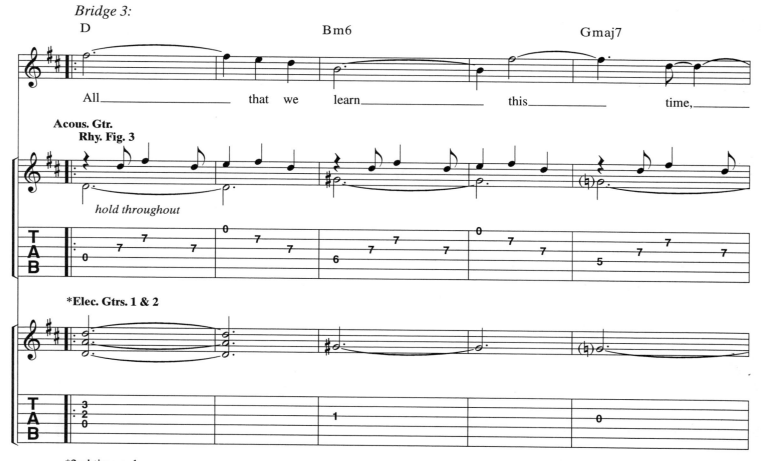

*2nd time only.

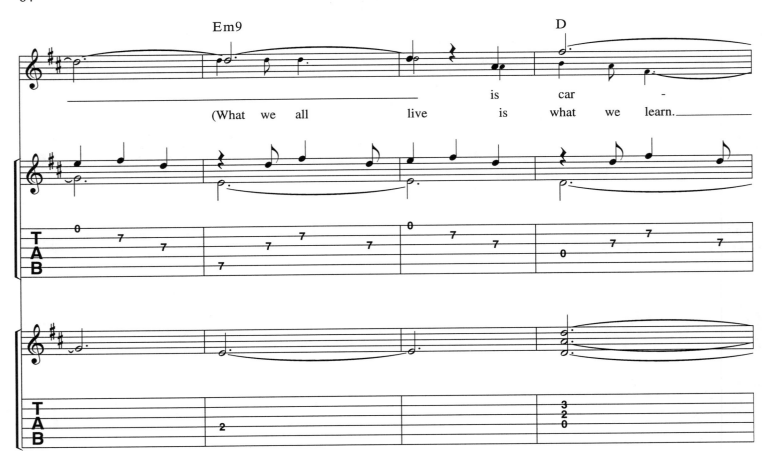

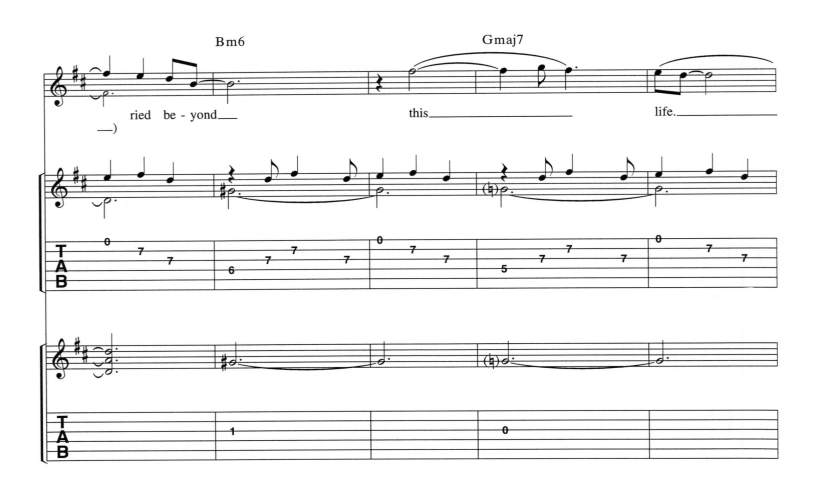

66

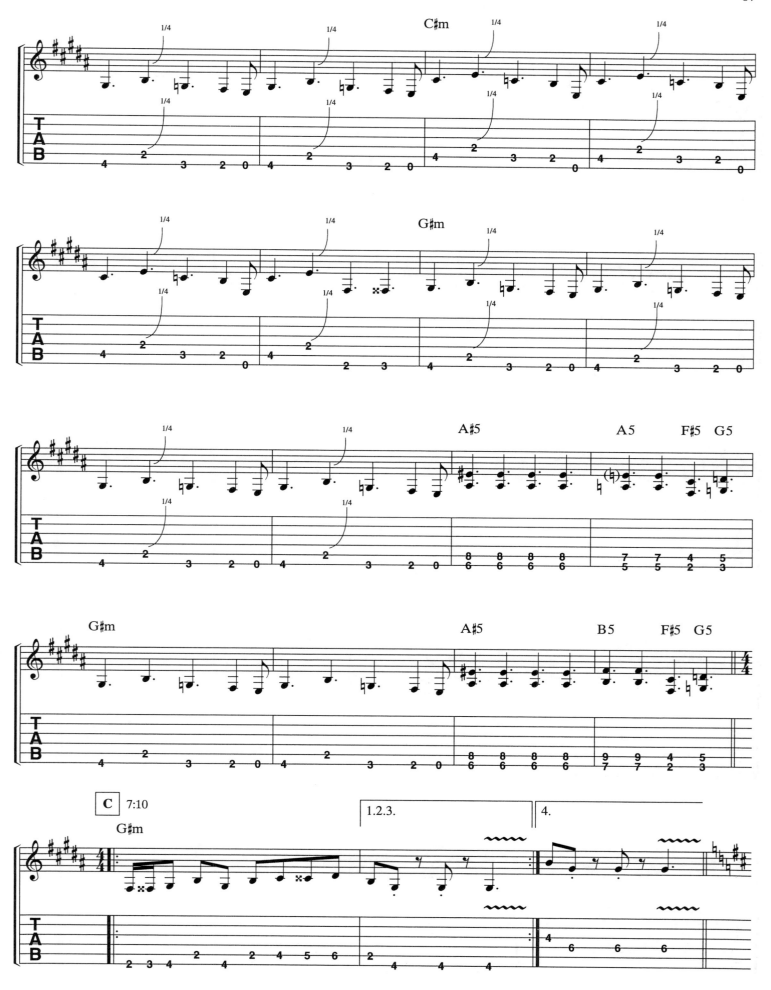

68

Guitar Solo:

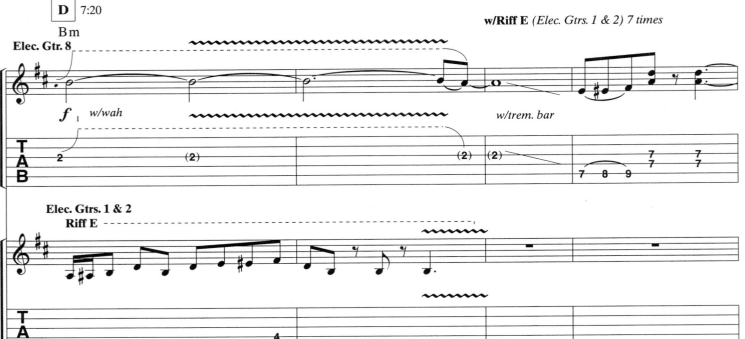

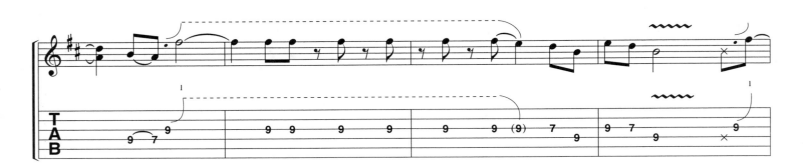

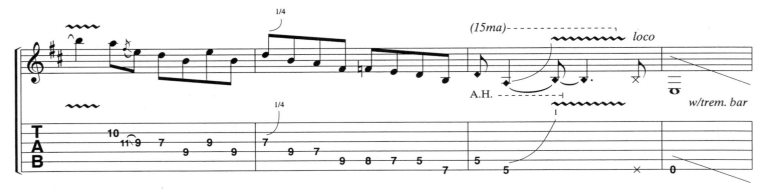

Scene Four: Beyond This Life - 33 - 22
0441B

Far Too Fat - 3/25/07

Strange Deja Vu
Stops: C#m | A | E/G# | F# | D | C# | Bm | F# | D | C# | B | E | Chorus

Rocket Queen (Eb)

18 and Life
Verse 2 (2nd half): A F# G A-B
Bridge: E B A B

Acid Rain (7)

Nothing Else Matters

TNT

I'll Stand By You
Verse: D F#m G B -A || D F#m G Bm-A
Prechorus: |: F# Bm :| G A
Chorus: D Bm Am7 D || F G
Verse: C Em F C-G || C Em F Am G
Prechorus: |: Em Am :| F G
Interlude: D Bm G Em Bm A
Bridge: F#m Bm Em G-A

Sugar (7)

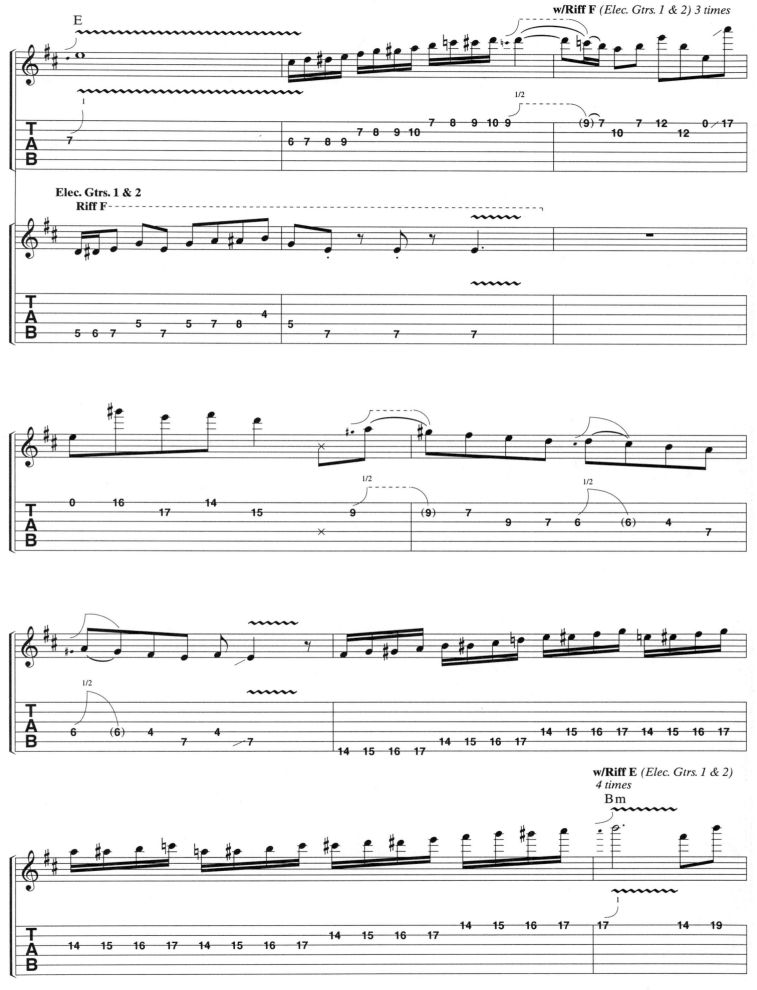

Scene Four: Beyond This Life - 33 - 23
0441B

70

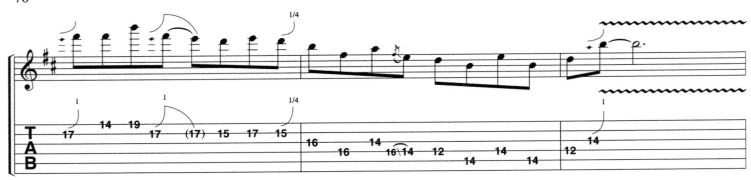

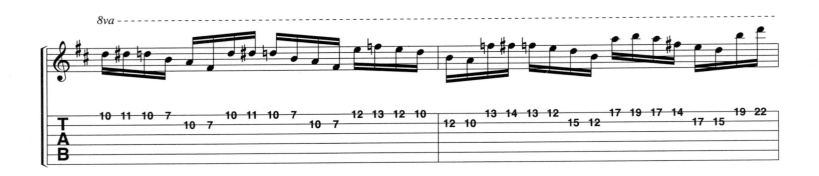

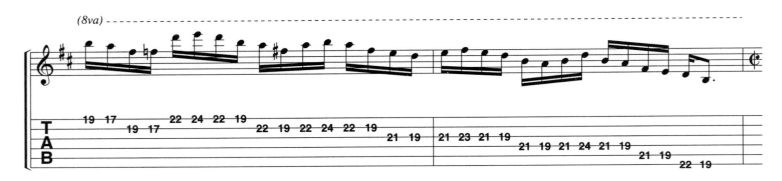

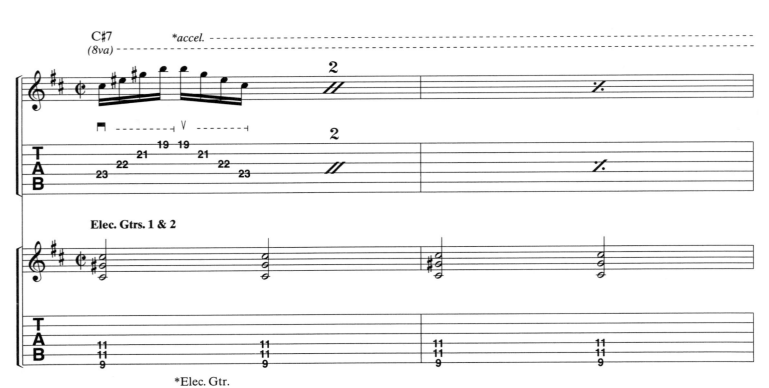

C#7

Elec. Gtrs. 1 & 2

*Elec. Gtr.

Scene Four: Beyond This Life - 33 - 24
0441B

F 9:06

Elec. Gtr. 9
* G#m

*Chord implied by bass gtr.

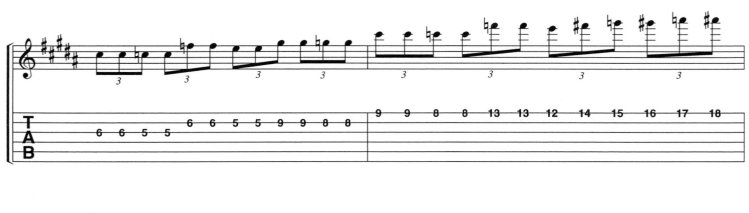

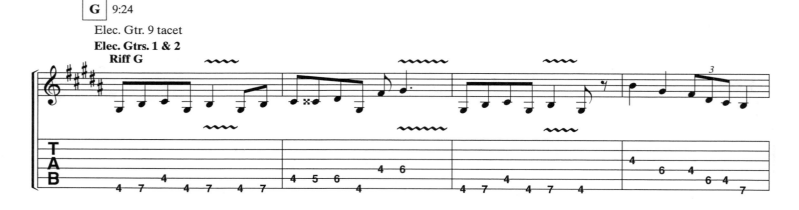

Scene Four: Beyond This Life - 33 - 28
0441B

w/Riff G *(Elec. Gtrs. 1 & 2)*

Elec. Gtr. 10

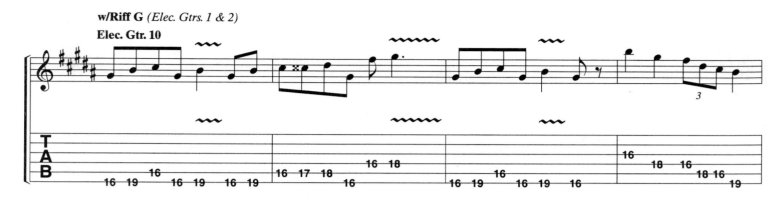

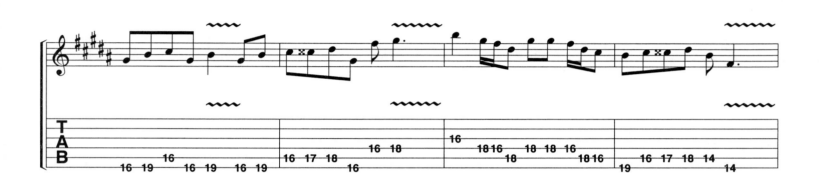

Elec. Gtr. 10 tacet

C#m

Elec. Gtr. 8

Elec. Gtrs. 1 & 2

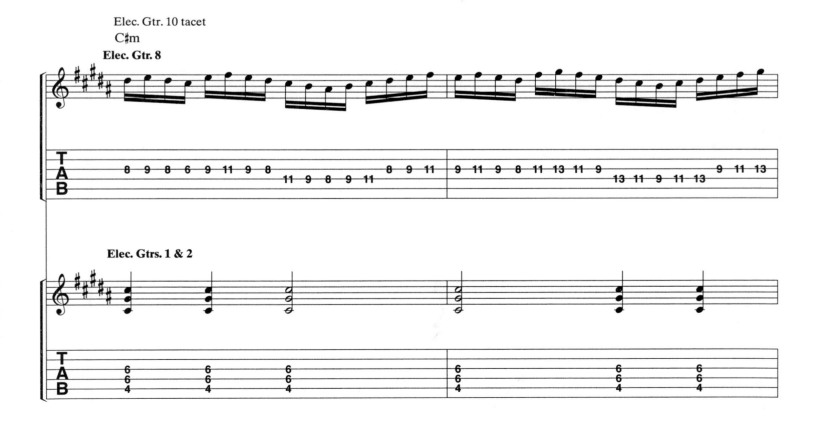

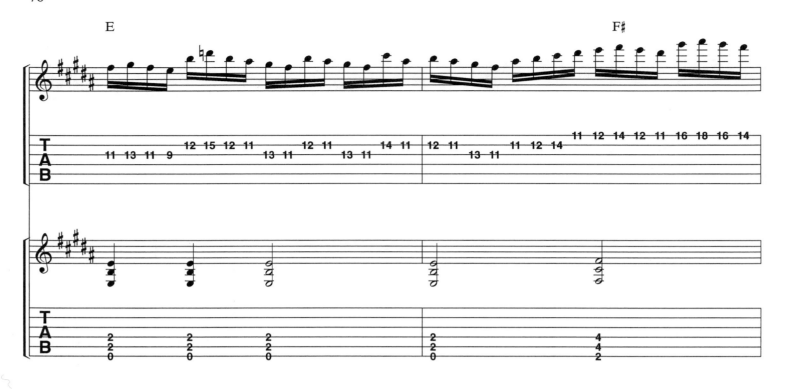

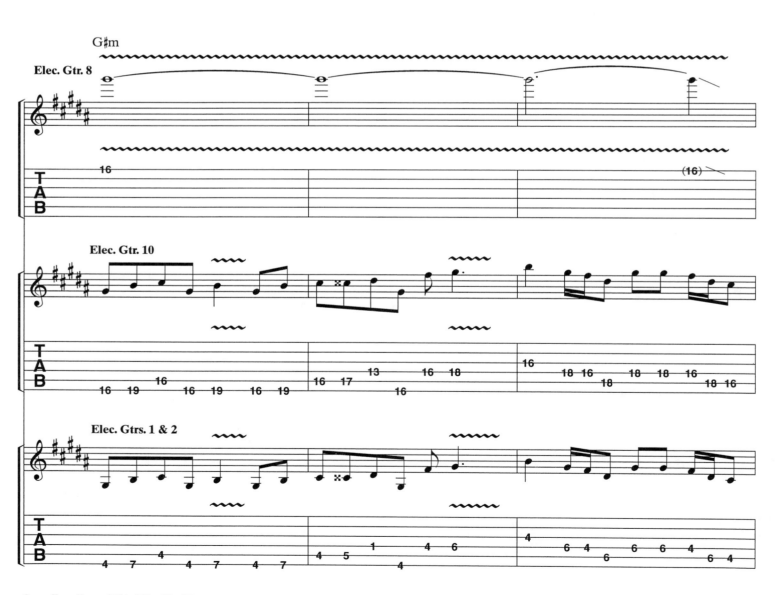

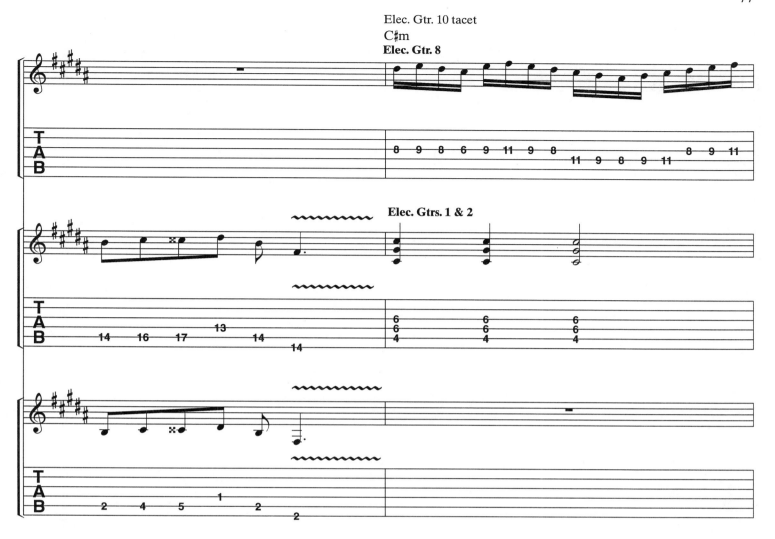

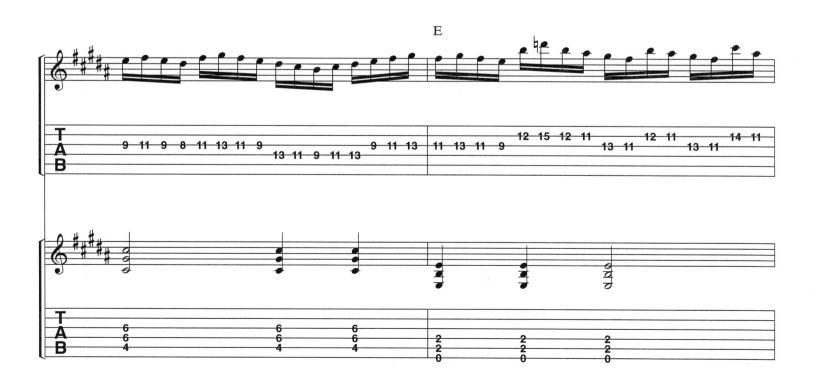

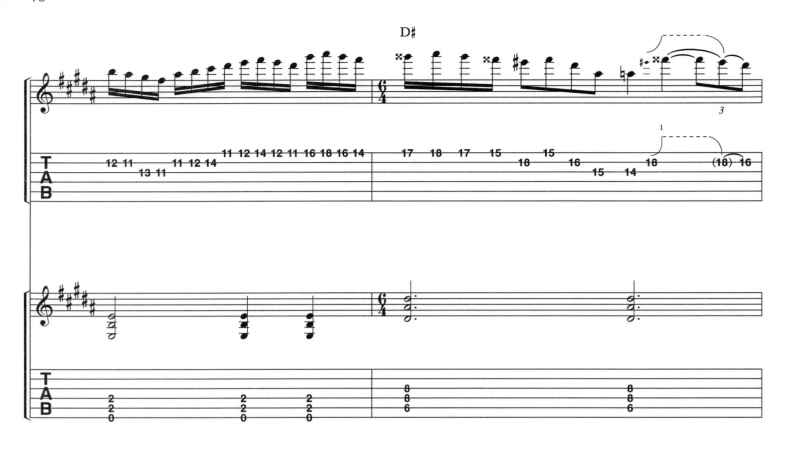

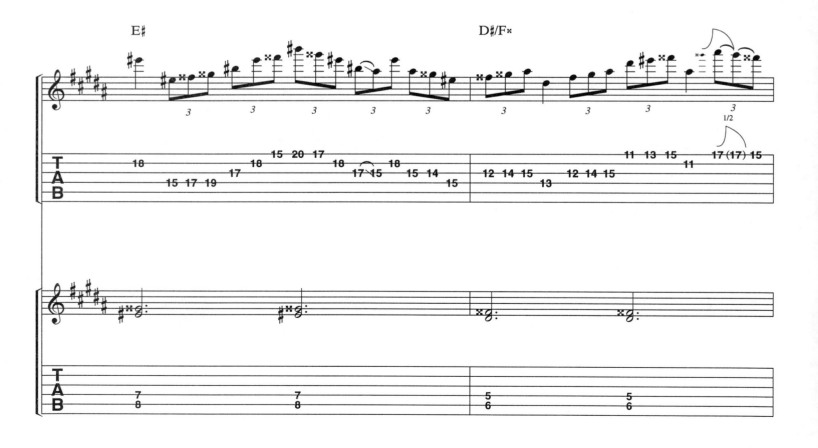

A/C#

D.S 𝄋 al Coda

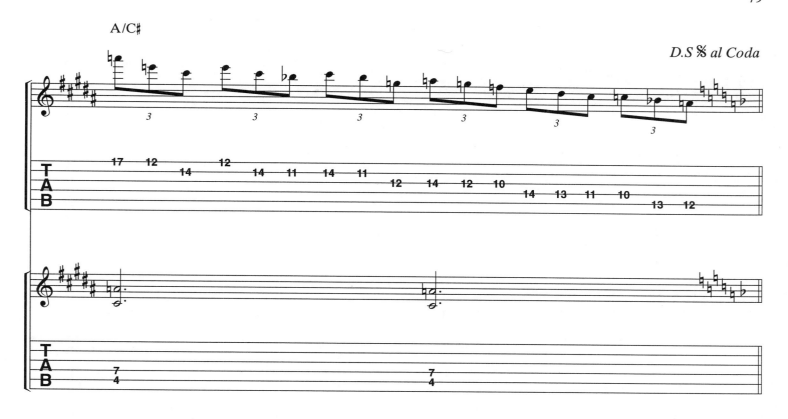

Coda

w/Rhy. Fig. 3 (*Acous. Gtr.*)

D   Bm6   Gmaj7   Em9

Elec. Gtrs. 1 & 2

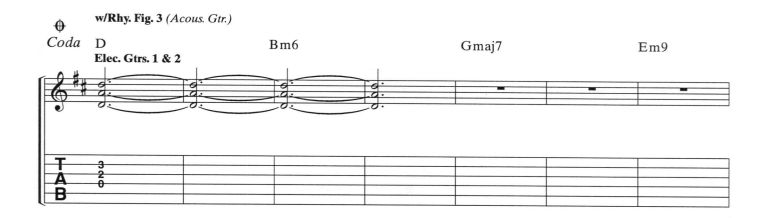

D   Bm6

Gmaj7   D/A   D

rit.   **Acous. Gtr.**

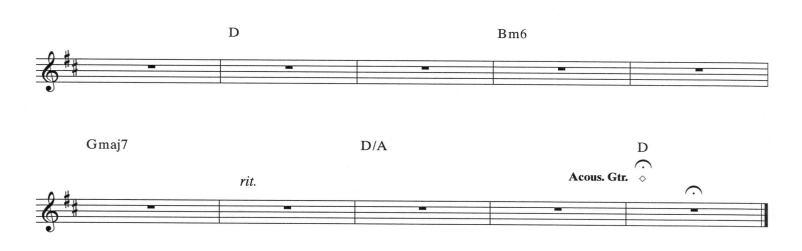

SCENE FIVE: THROUGH HER EYES

Music by DREAM THEATER
Lyrics by JOHN PETRUCCI

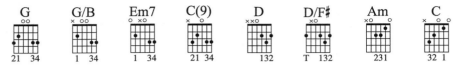

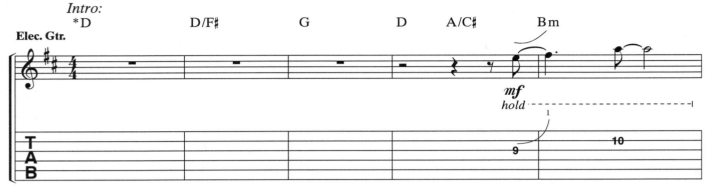

*Chords played by synth.

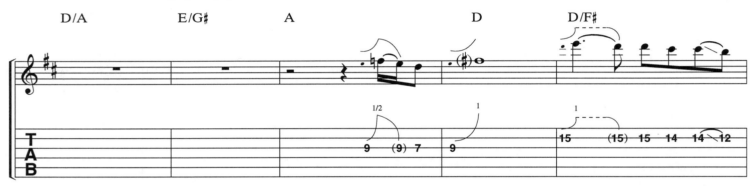

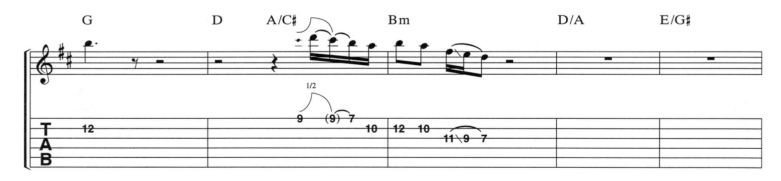

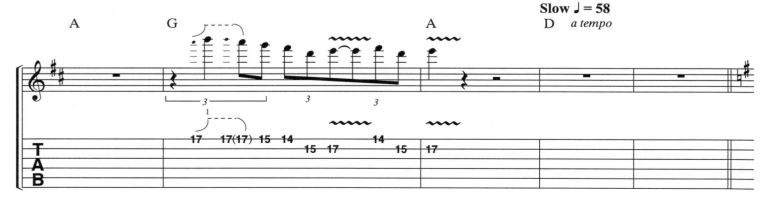

Scene Five: Through Her Eyes - 4 - 1
0441B

Em7   D   *D.S. %% al Coda*

this   felt   just   the   same._____

Coda

Em7   D

The door has o - pened wide,___   I'm turn - ing with__ the tide,__

Outro:
w/ad lib. vocal
Acous. Gtr. cont. rhy. simile

C   Am   G   G/B

___   look-ing   through_ her   eyes.___

Elec. Gtr.

Em7   C(9)   G

Repeat and fade

D   Em7   C(9)

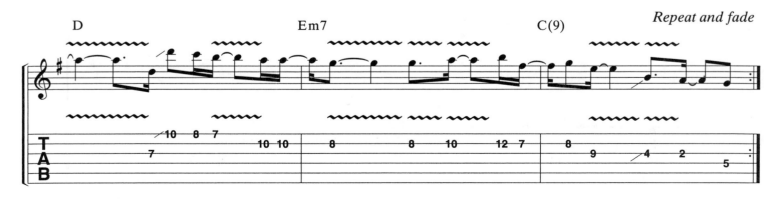

Scene Five: Through Her Eyes - 4 - 4
0441B

SCENE SIX: HOME

All gtrs. w/dropped D tuning:
⑥ = D

Music by DREAM THEATER
Lyrics by MIKE PORTNOY

Moderately ♩ = 88

Intro:

  :00

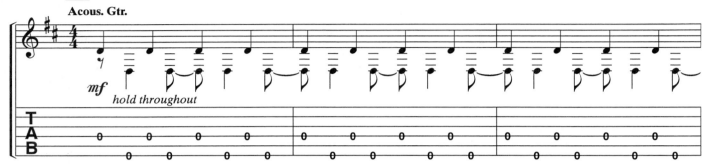

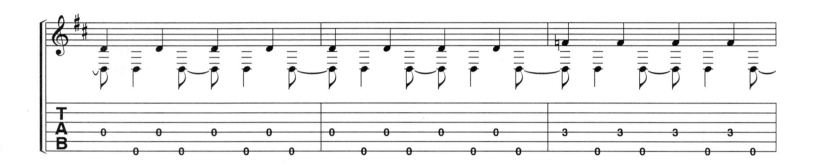

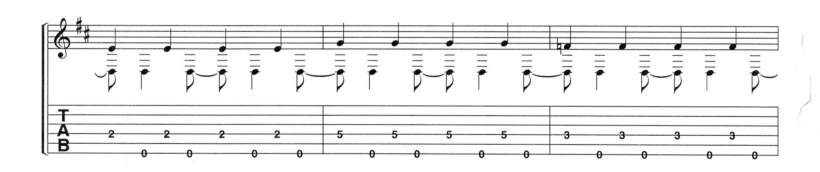

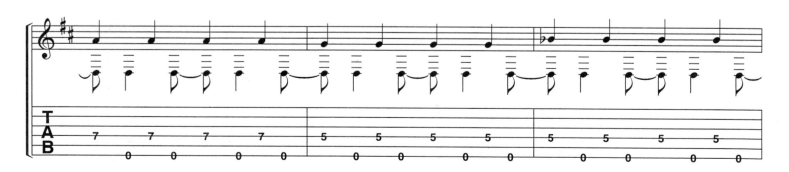

Scene Six: Home - 29 - 1
0441B

Bass gtr. enters

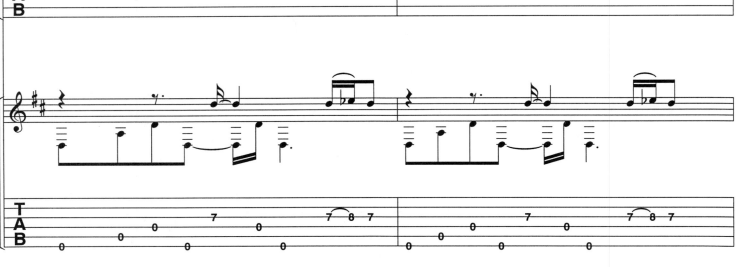

88

Drums enter

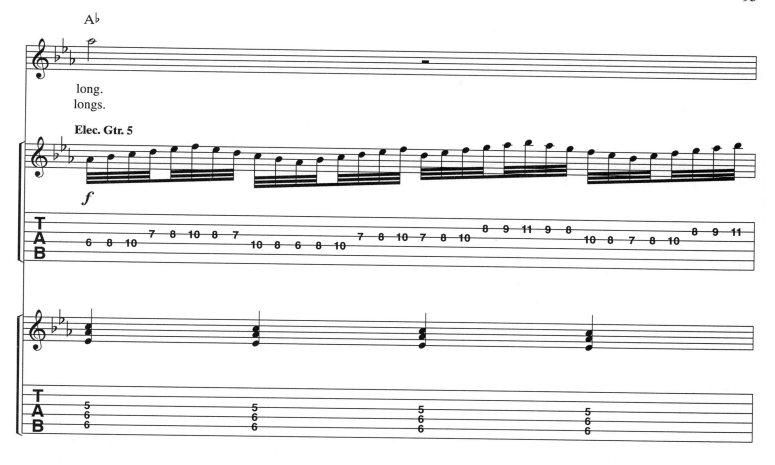

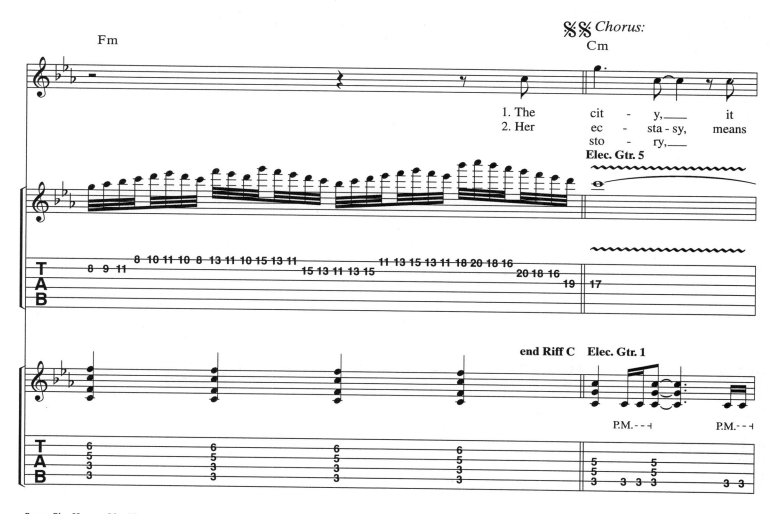

calls to me.
so much to me.
it holds the key.

Dec - a - dent scenes from my mem - 'ry.
E - ven de - ceiv - ing my own blood.
Un - lock - ing dreams from my mem - 'ry.

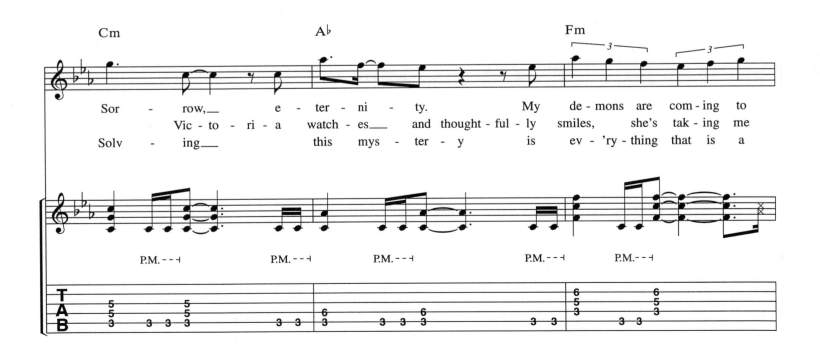

Sor - row,___ e - ter - ni - ty. My de - mons are com - ing to
Vic - to - ri - a watch - es___ and thought - ful - ly smiles, she's tak - ing me
Solv - ing___ this mys - ter - y is ev - 'ry - thing that is a

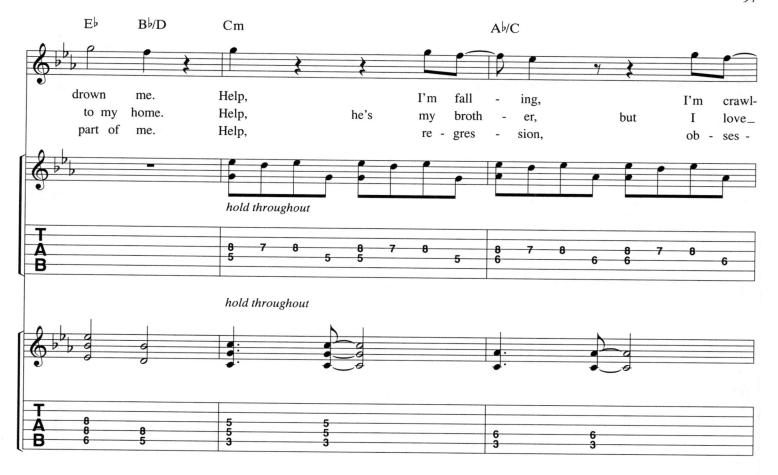

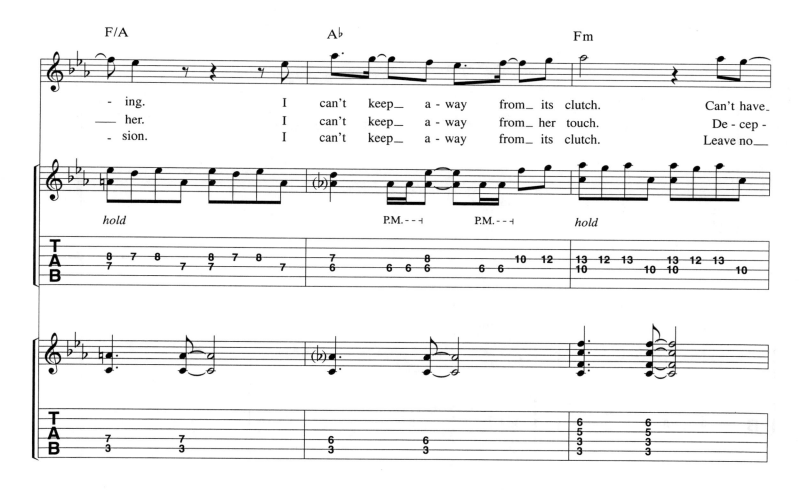

98

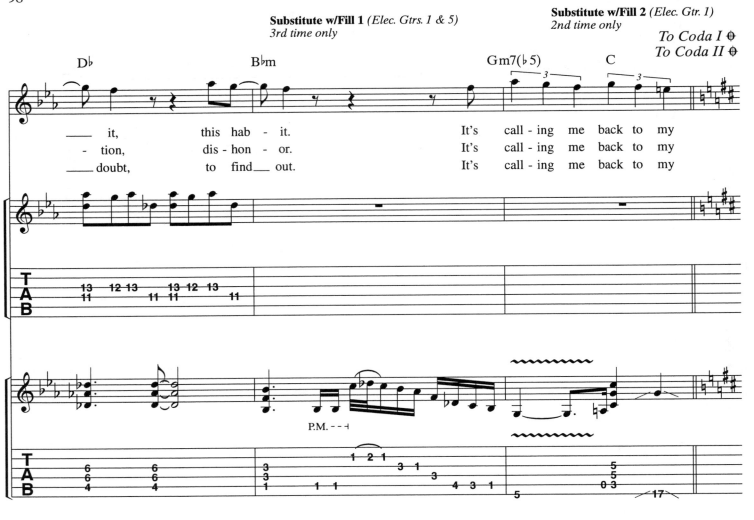

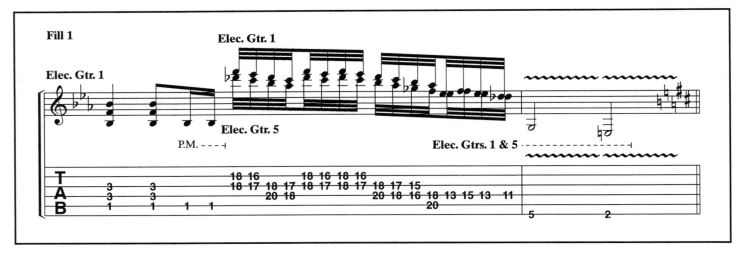

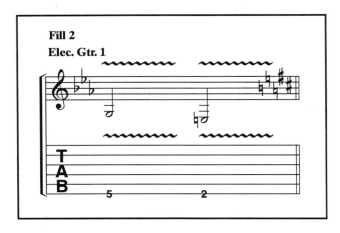

w/Riff A *(Elec. Gtrs. 1 & 6)*

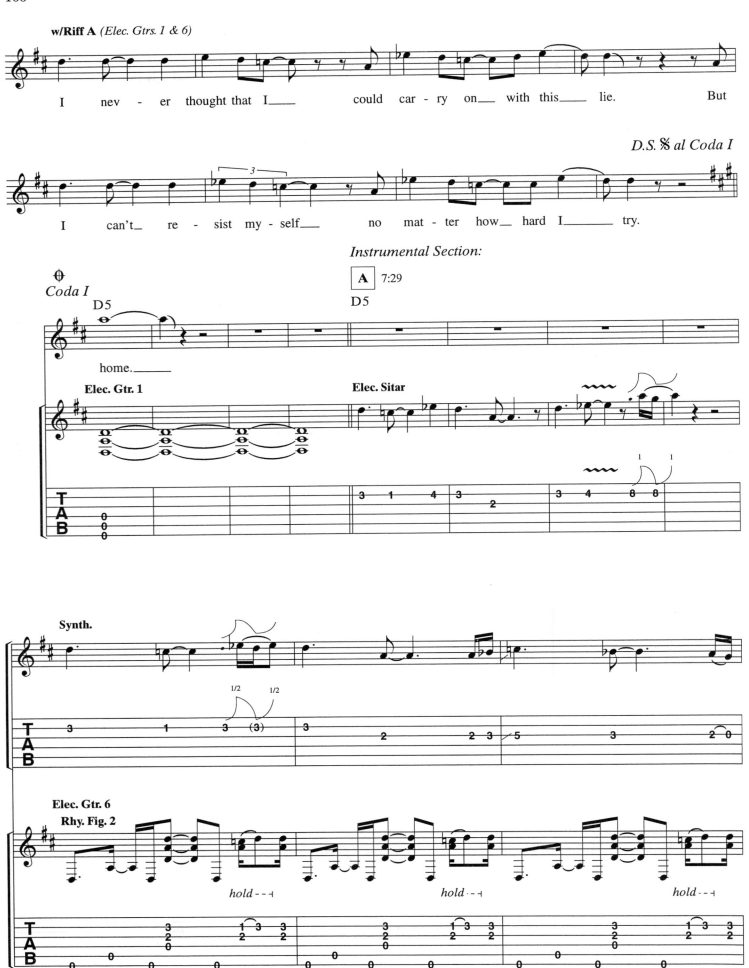

I nev - er thought that I___ could car - ry on___ with this___ lie. But

D.S. % al Coda I

I can't___ re - sist my - self___ no mat - ter how___ hard I_____ try.

Instrumental Section:

Coda I

A 7:29

D5

D5

home._____

Elec. Gtr. 1

Elec. Sitar

Synth.

1/2   1/2

Elec. Gtr. 6
Rhy. Fig. 2

hold - - ⌐   *hold - - ⌐*   *hold - - ⌐*

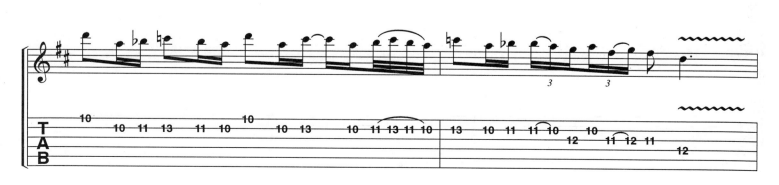

102

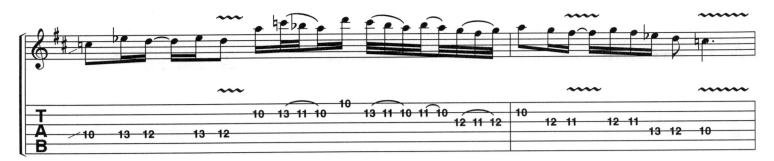

Elec. Gtr. 6 tacet

Elec. Gtr. 1 -
Riff D

w/**Riff D** (*Elec. Gtr. 1*) *3 times*

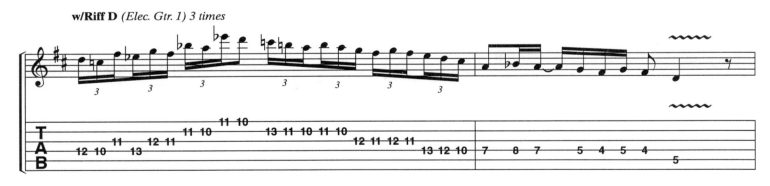

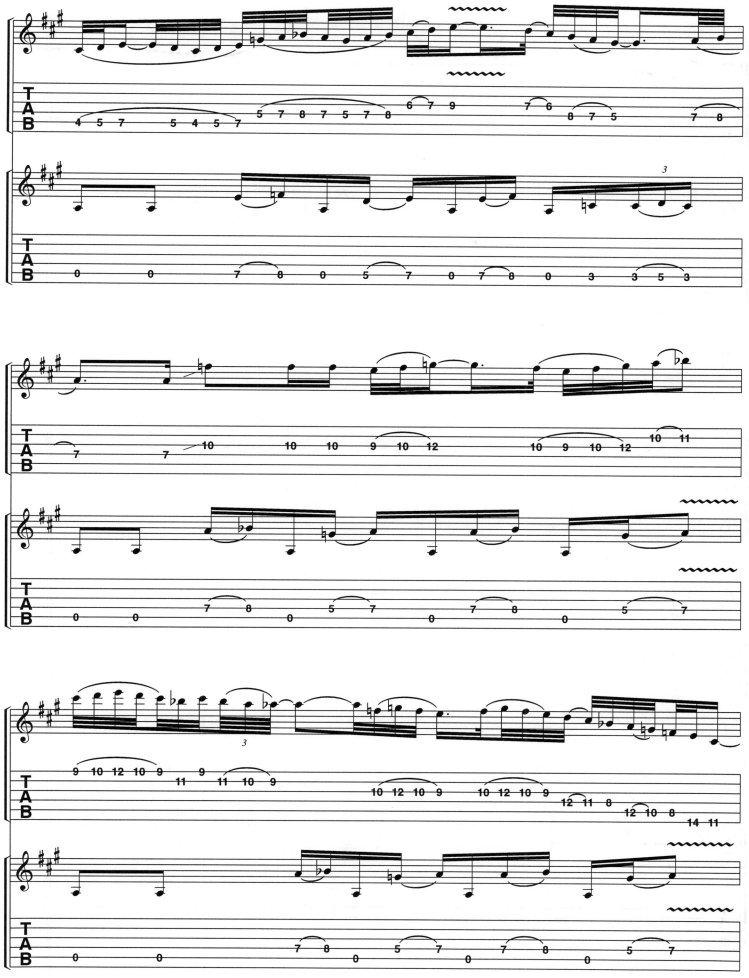

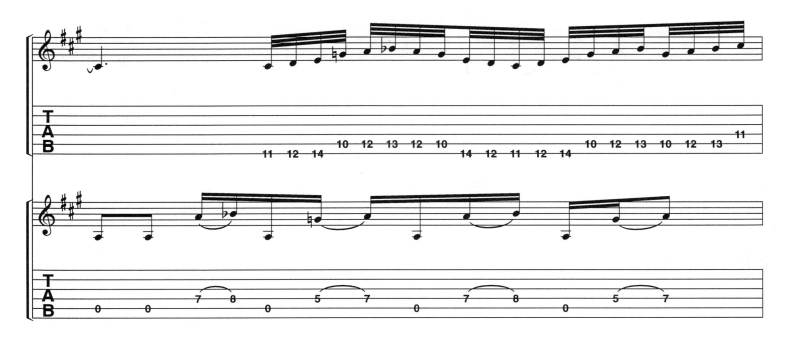

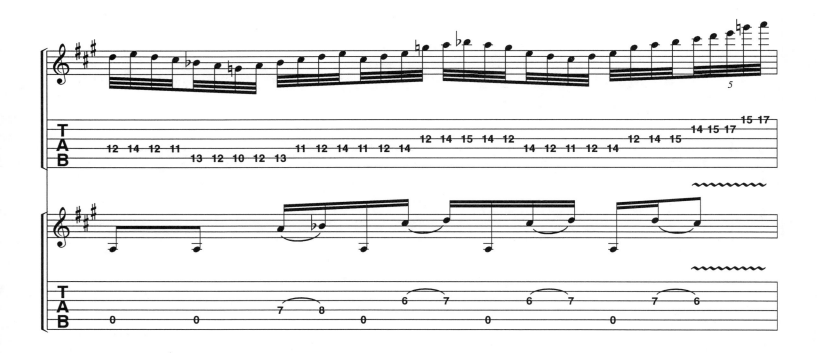

w/Riff C *(Elec. Gtr. 1)*

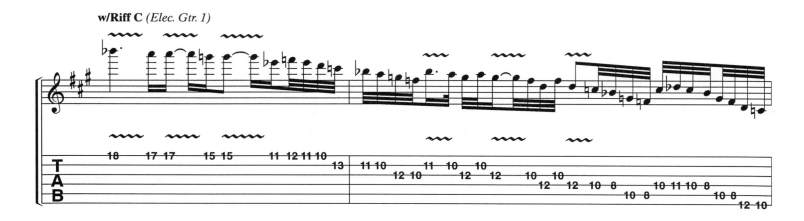

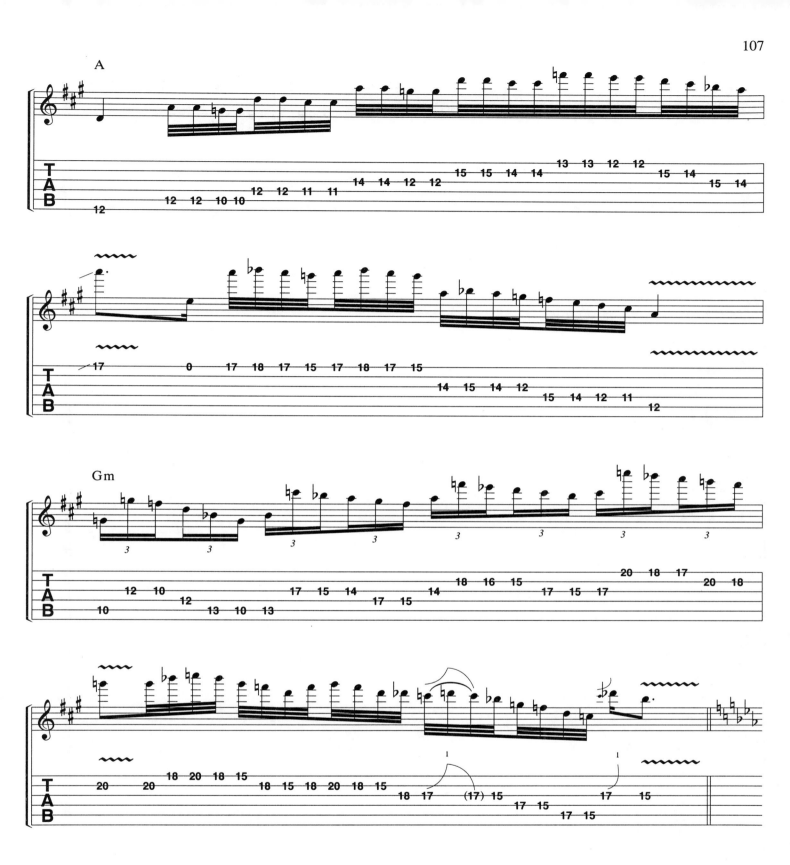

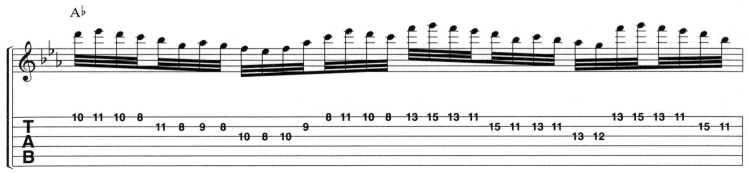

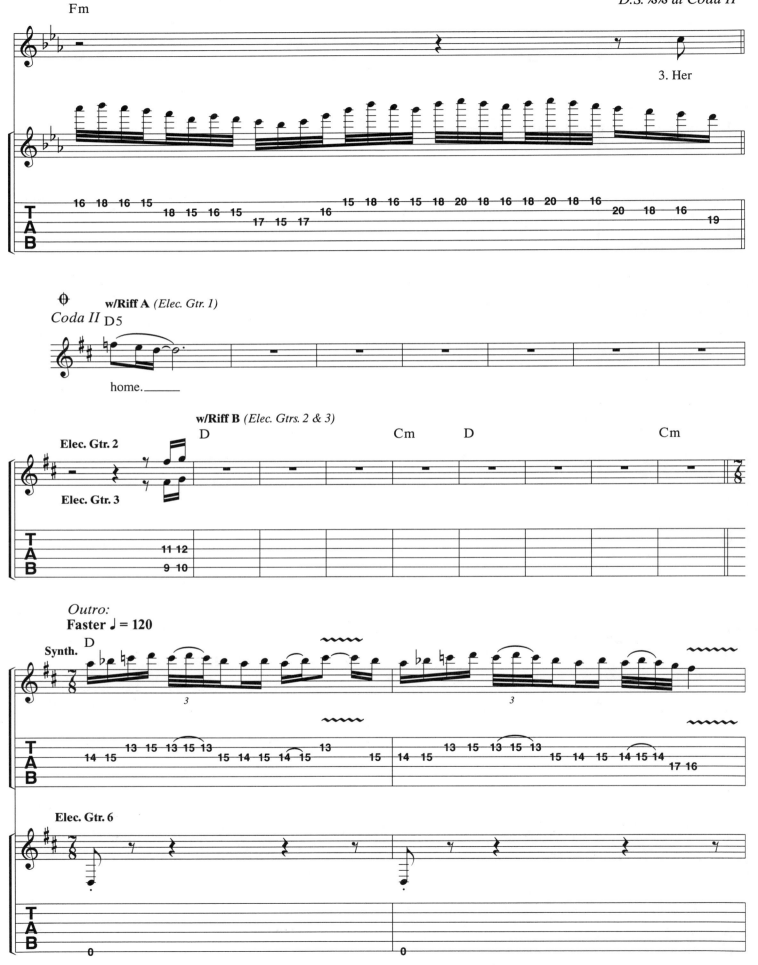

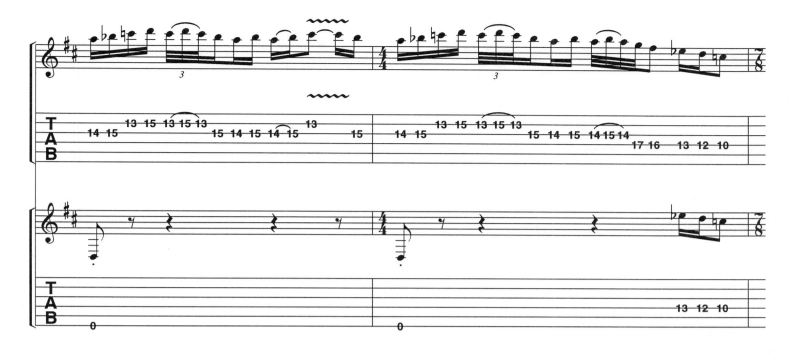

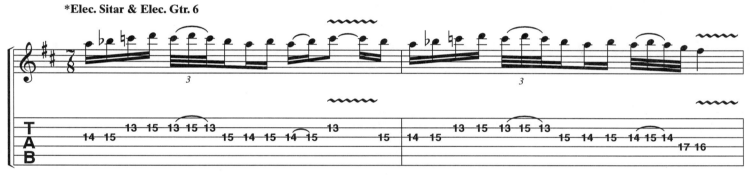

*Elec. Sitar & Elec. Gtr. 6

*Elec. Sitar & Elec. Gtr. 6 play unison.

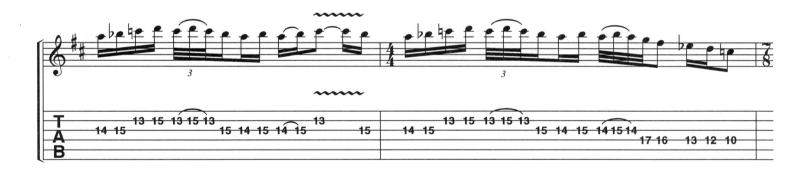

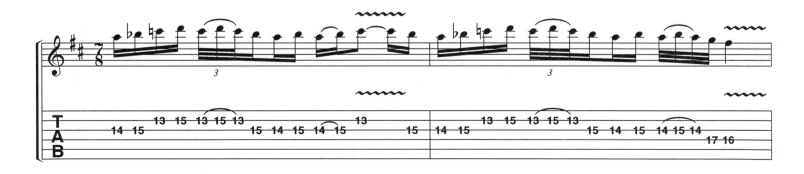

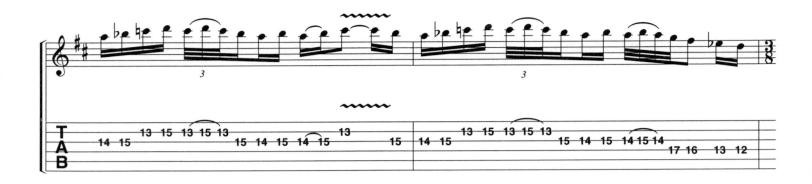

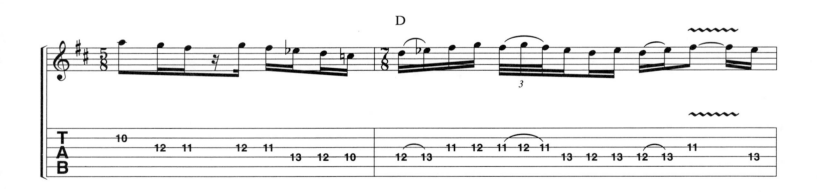

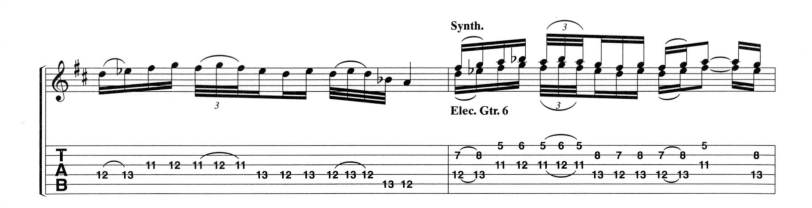

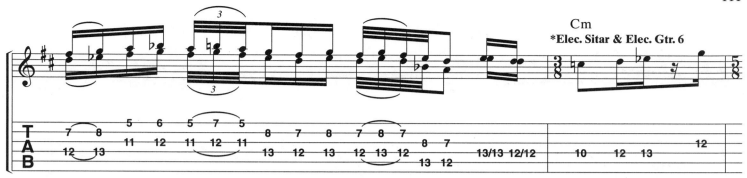

Cm
*Elec. Sitar & Elec. Gtr. 6

*Elec. Sitar & Elec. Gtr. 6 play unison.

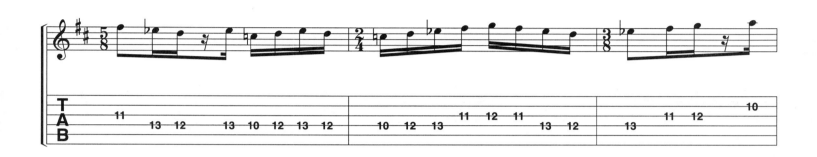

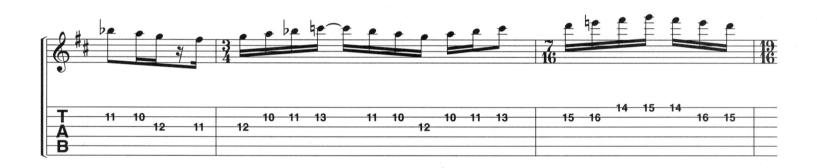

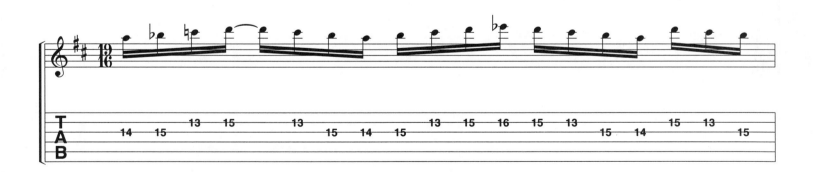

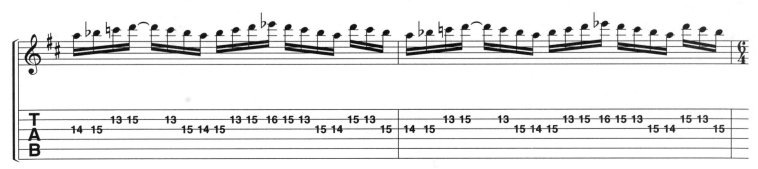

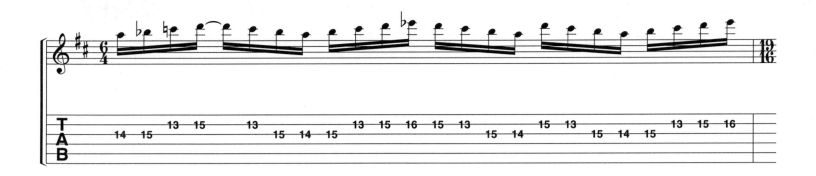

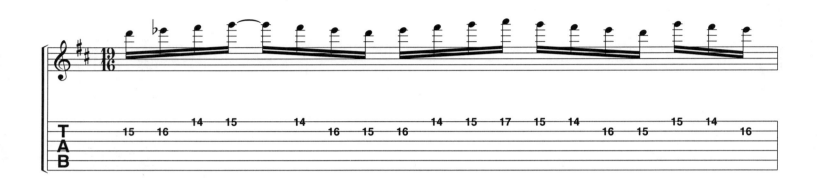

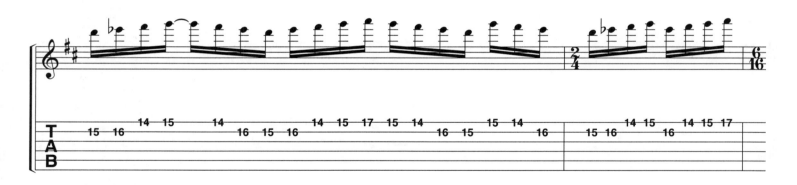

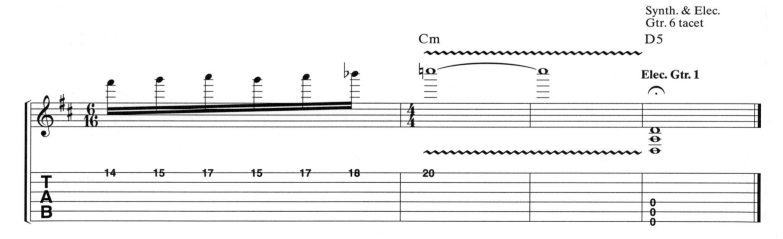

SCENE SEVEN: I. THE DANCE OF ETERNITY

Music by
DREAM THEATER

All gtrs. are 7-string elec. gtrs. in standard tuning:
⑦ = B

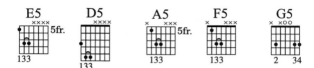

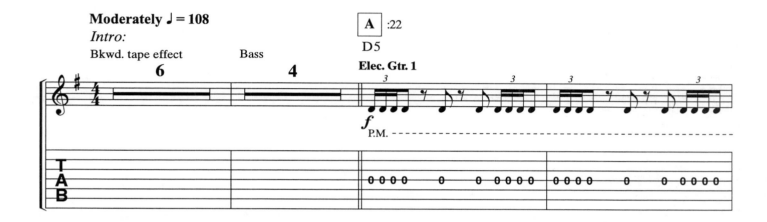

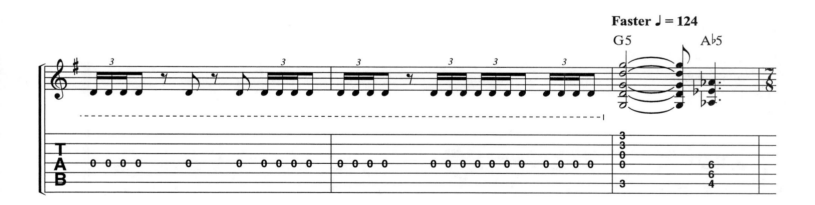

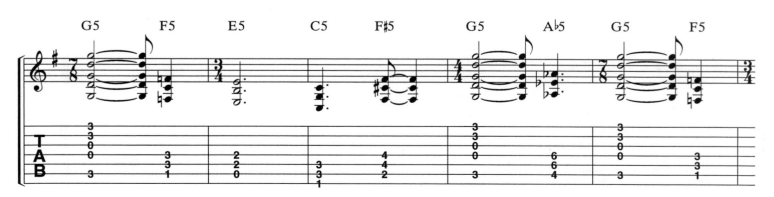

Scene Seven: I. The Dance of Eternity - 18 - 1
0441B

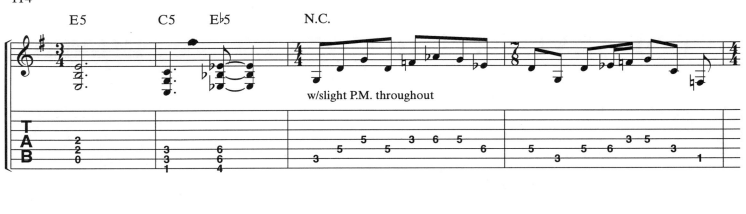

w/slight P.M. throughout

Scene Seven: I. The Dance of Eternity - 18 - 3
0441B

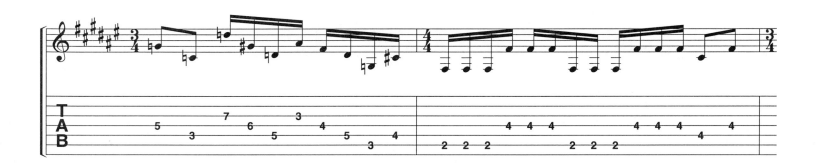

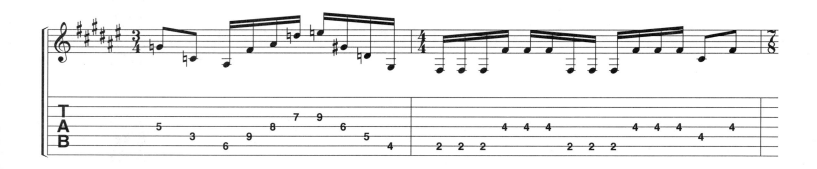

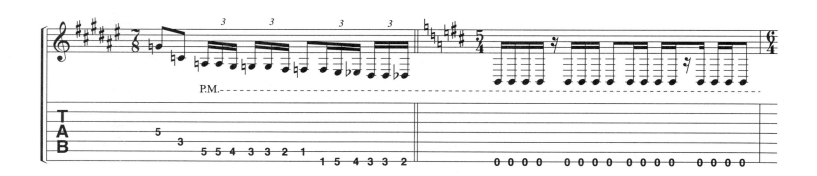

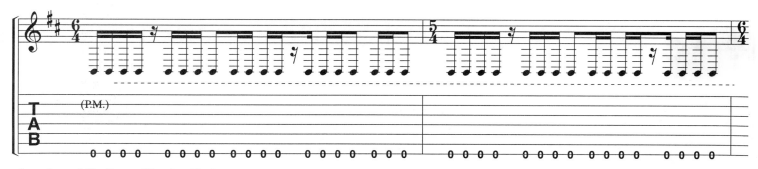

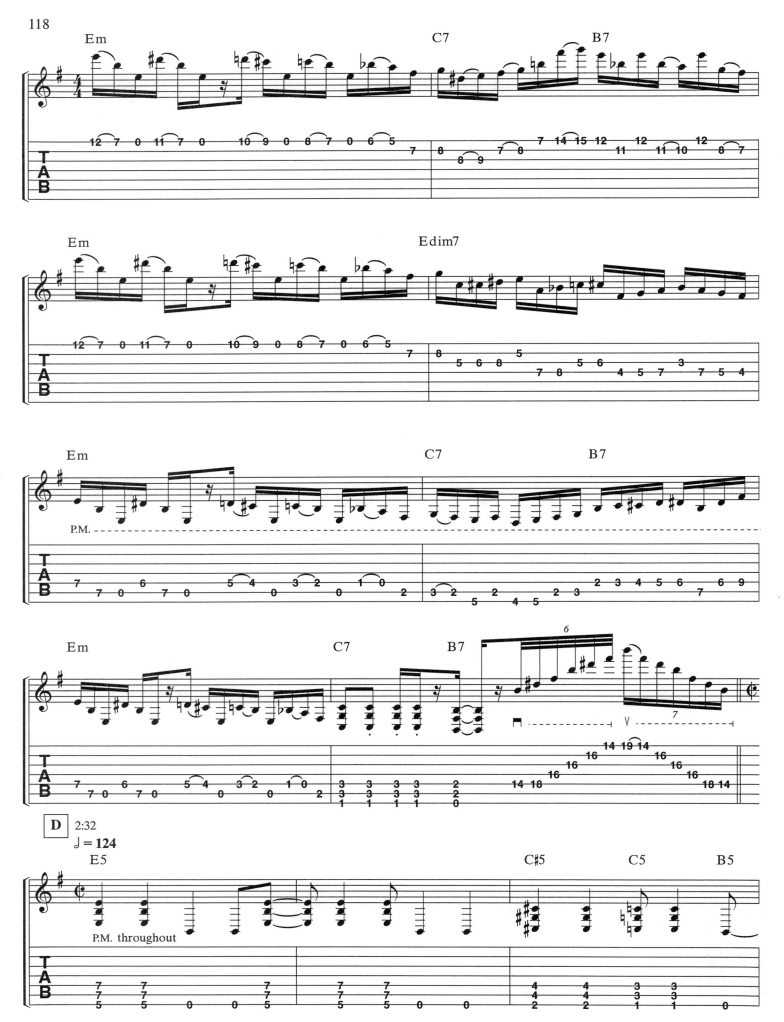

120

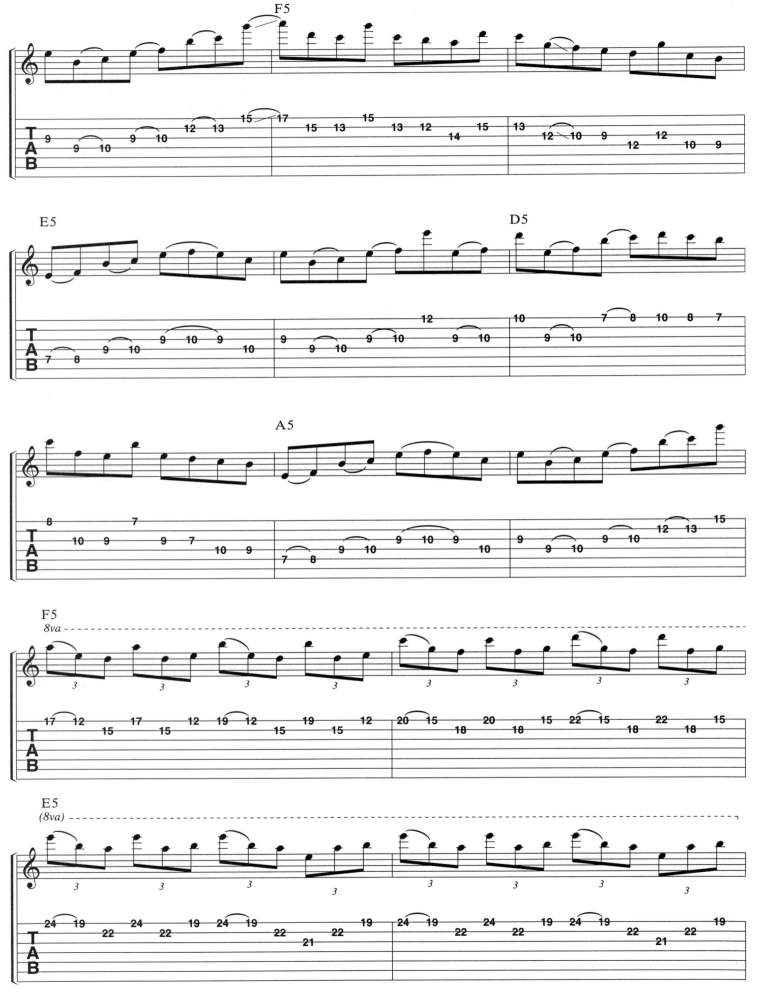

Scene Seven: I. The Dance of Eternity - 18 - 8
0441B

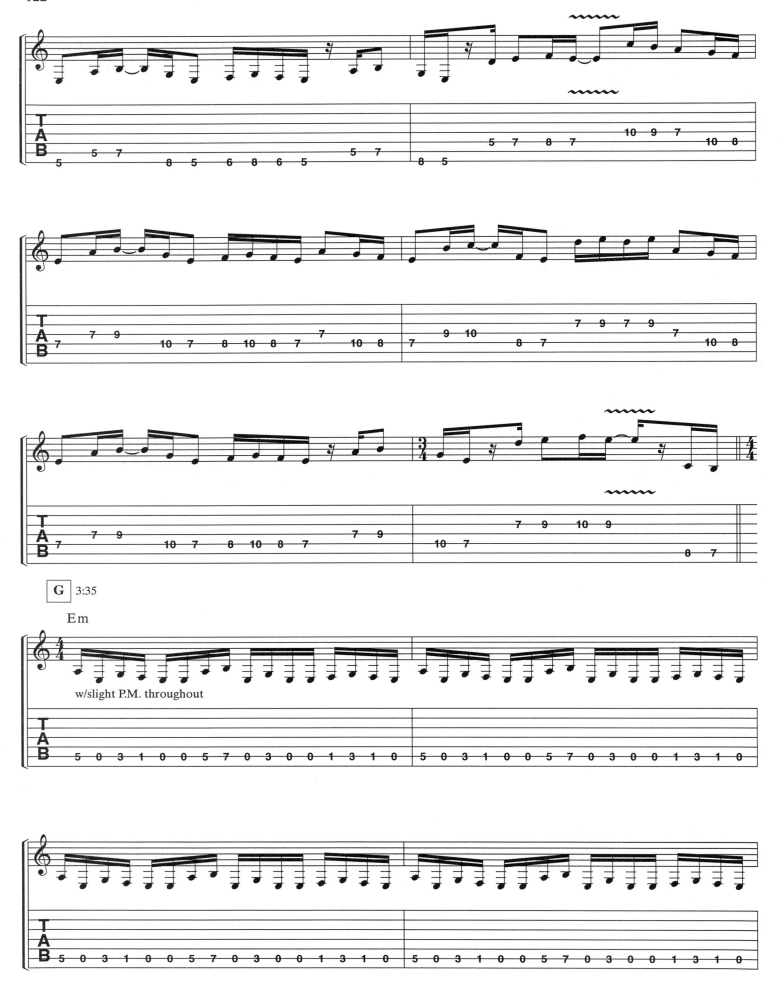

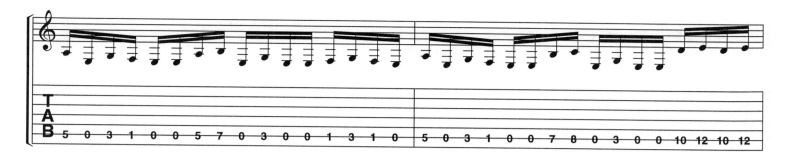

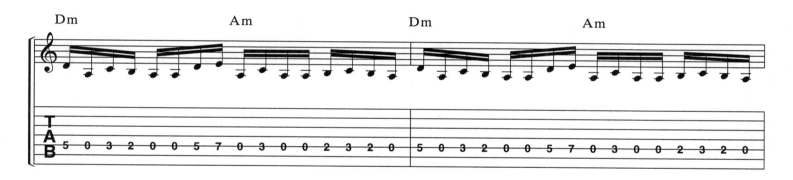

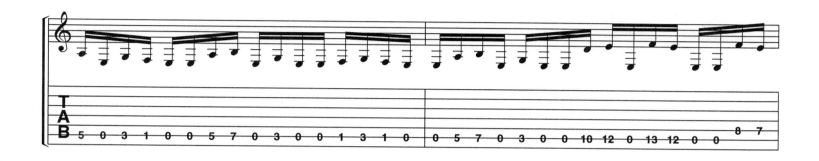

Scene Seven: I. The Dance of Eternity - 18 - 11
0441B

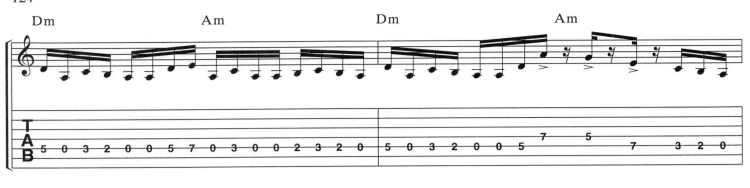

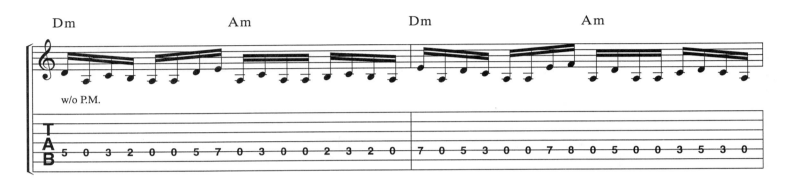

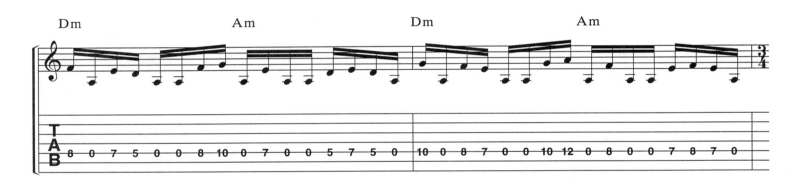

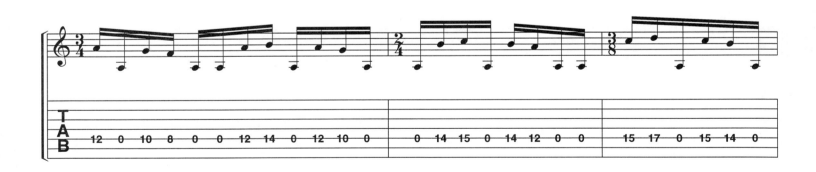

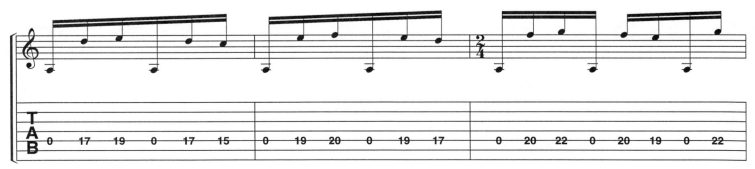

Scene Seven: I. The Dance of Eternity - 18 - 12
0441B

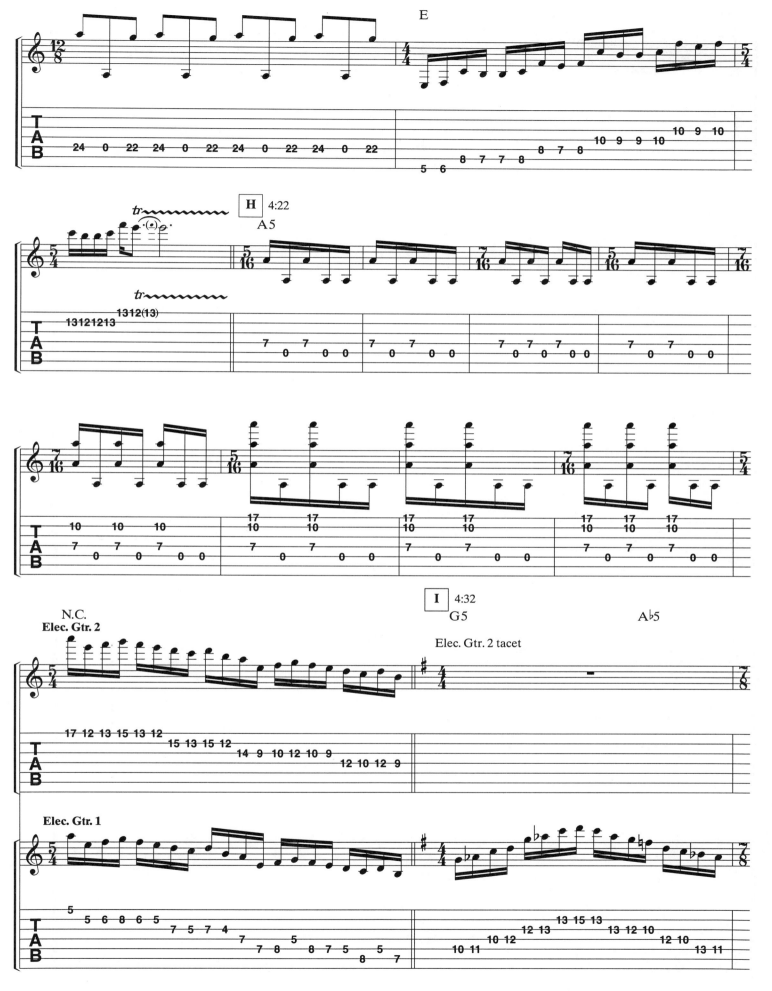

126

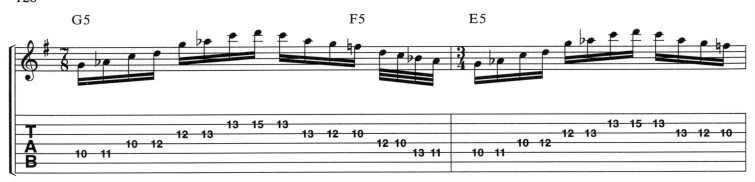

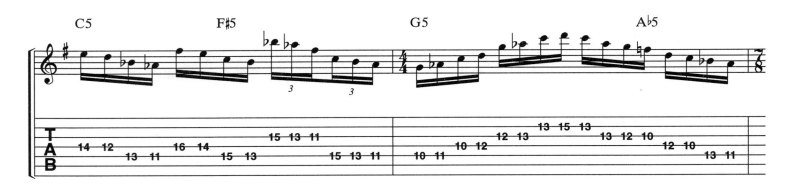

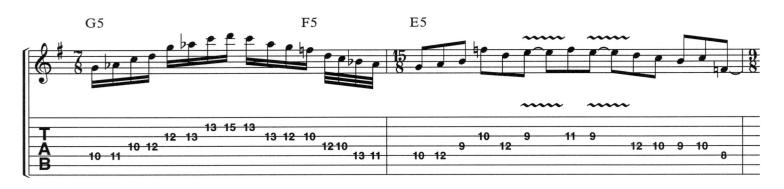

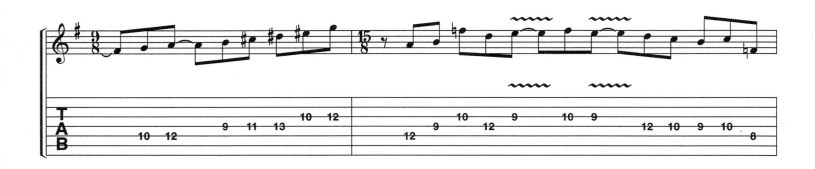

N.C.

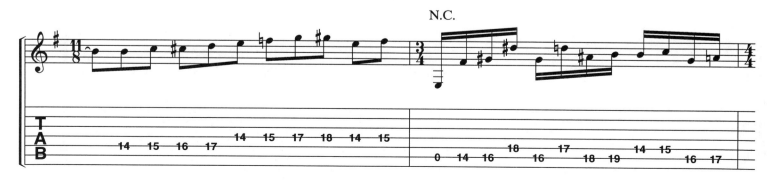

Scene Seven: I. The Dance of Eternity - 18 - 15
0441B

128

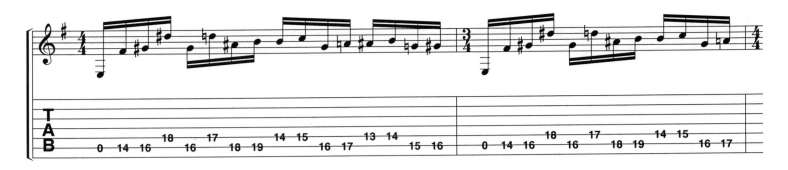

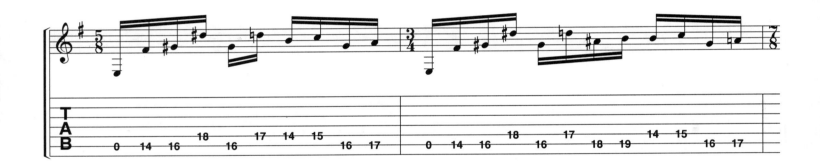

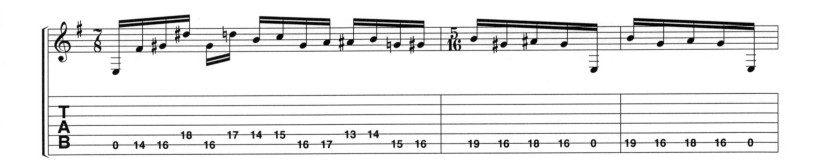

Scene Seven: I. The Dance of Eternity - 18 - 16
0441B

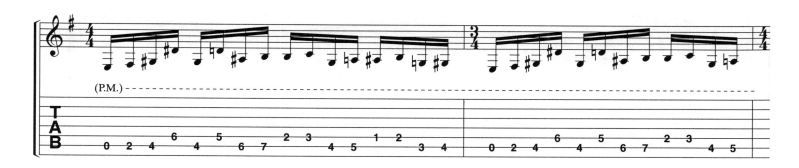

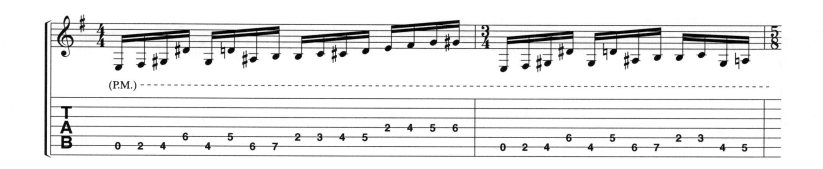

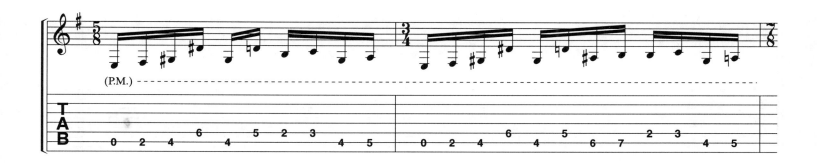

E

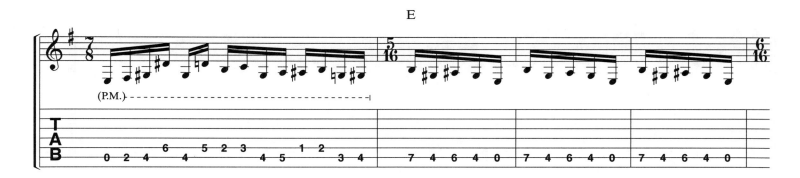

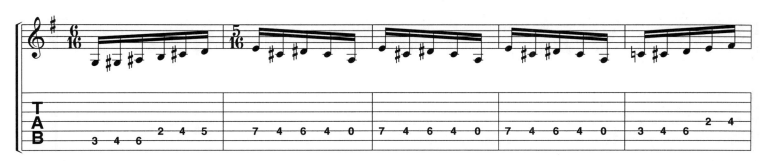

Scene Seven: I. The Dance of Eternity - 18 - 17
0441B

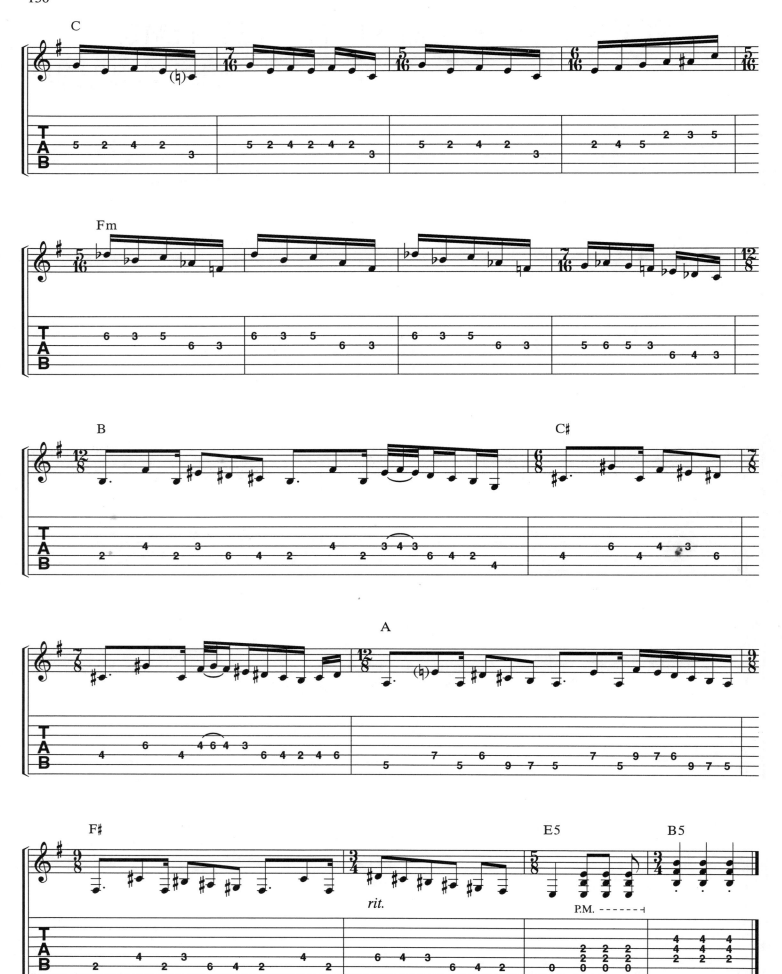

SCENE SEVEN: II. ONE LAST TIME

Music by DREAM THEATER
Lyrics by JAMES LABRIE

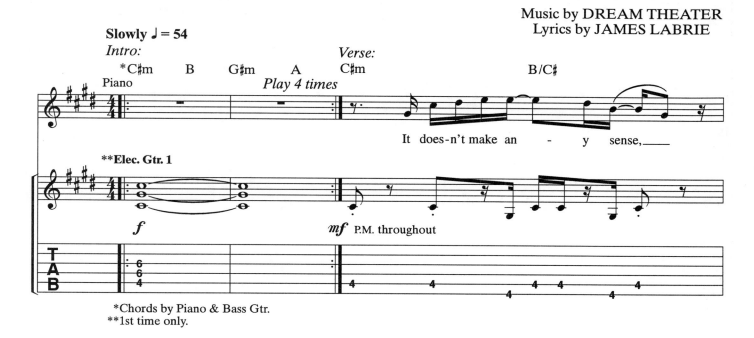

*Chords by Piano & Bass Gtr.
**1st time only.

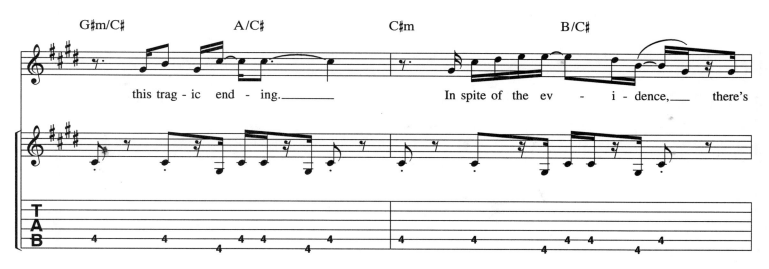

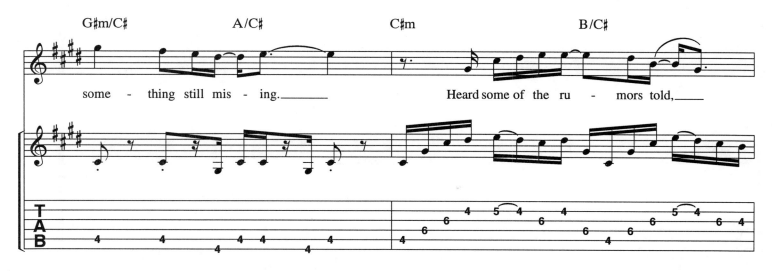

Scene Seven: II. One Last Time - 8 - 1
0441B

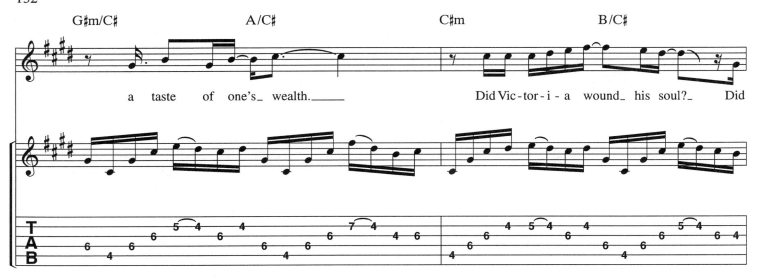

a taste of one's wealth._____ Did Vic-tor-i-a wound_ his soul?_ Did

Chorus:
Elec. Gtr. 1 tacet

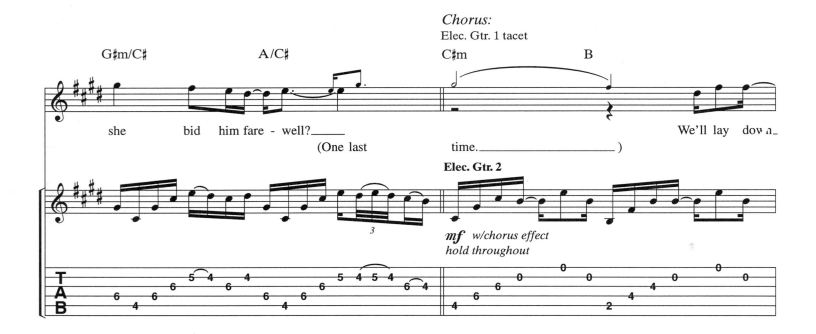

she bid him fare - well?_____ We'll lay dow n_

(One last time._____)

Elec. Gtr. 2

mf *w/chorus effect*
hold throughout

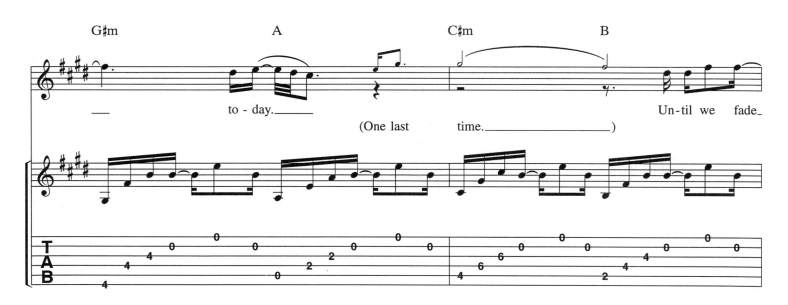

___ to - day._____ Un-til we fade_

(One last time._____)

134

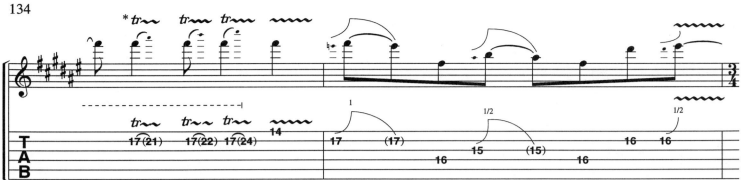

*Hold bend while trilling w/right hand index finger.

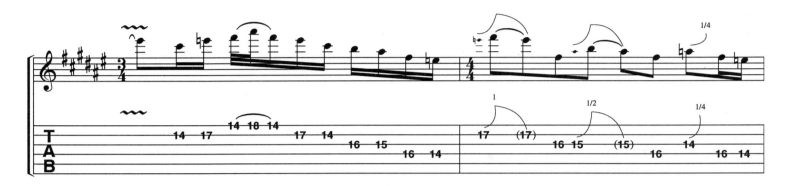

Bridge:

Asus2

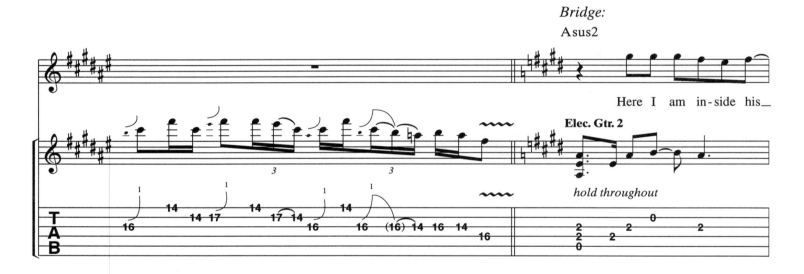

Here I am in-side his___

Elec. Gtr. 2

hold throughout

Bsus   Asus2   F#11

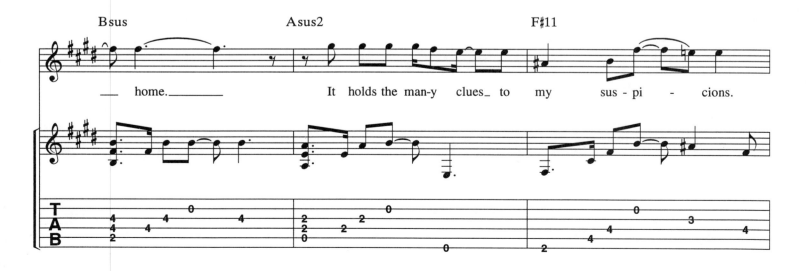

___ home._____   It holds the man-y clues_ to   my   sus - pi - cions.

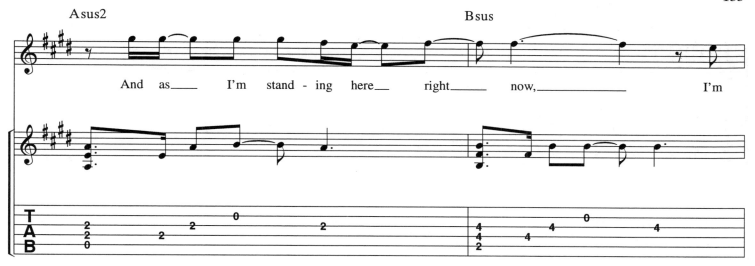

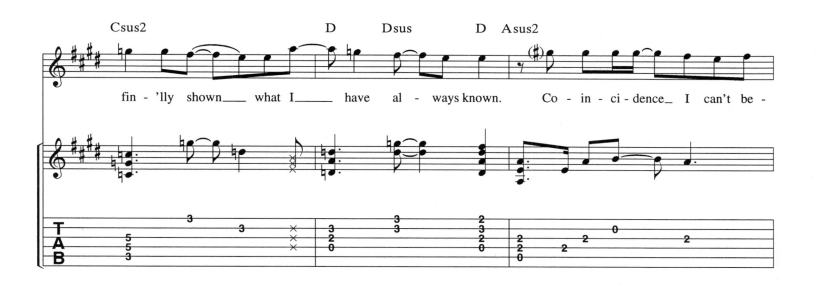

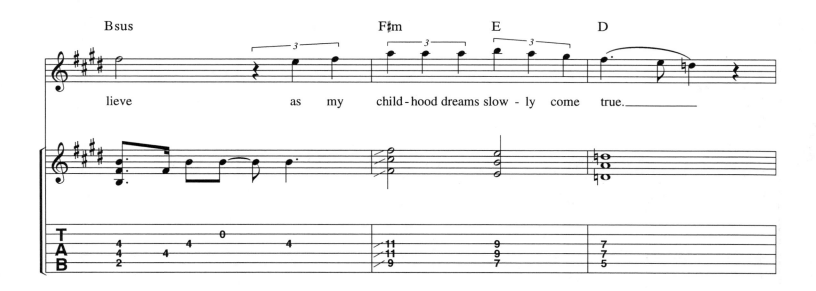

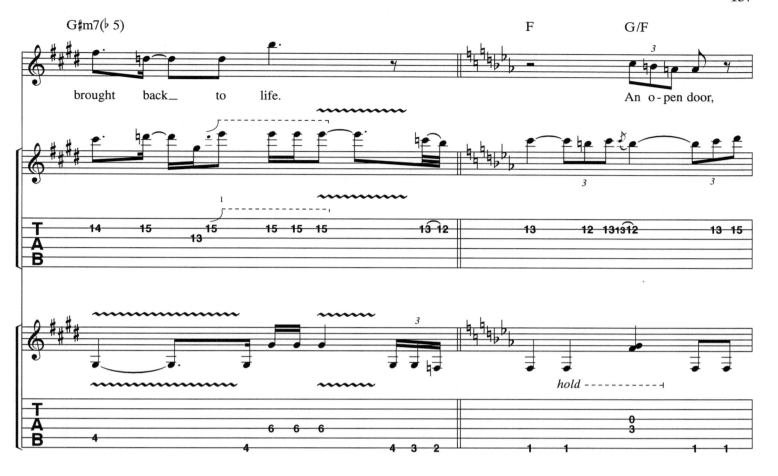

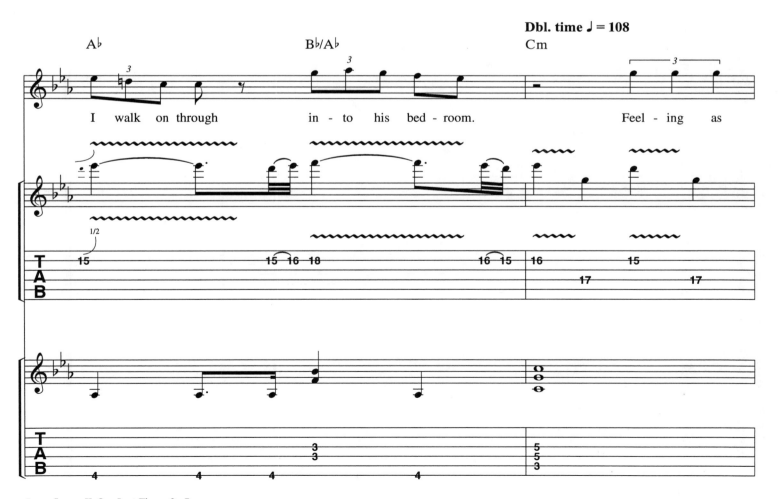

SCENE EIGHT: THE SPIRIT CARRIES ON

Music by DREAM THEATER
Lyrics by JOHN PETRUCCI

Verse 2:

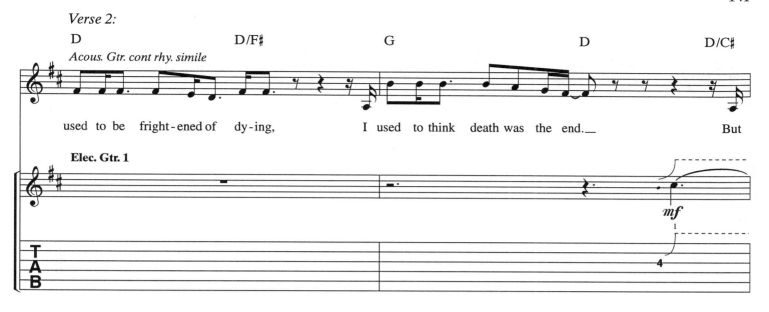

used to be fright-ened of dy-ing, I used to think death was the end.___ But

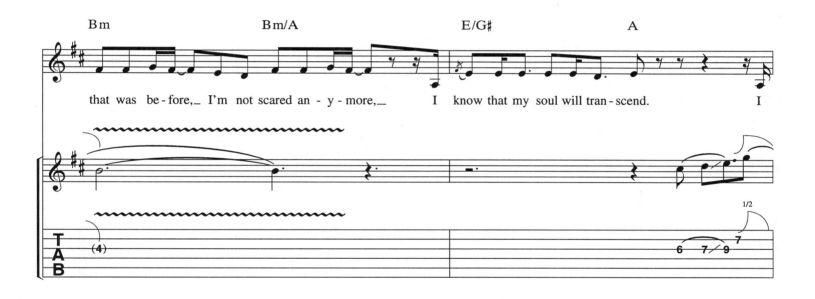

that was be-fore,_ I'm not scared an-y-more,_ I know that my soul will tran-scend. I

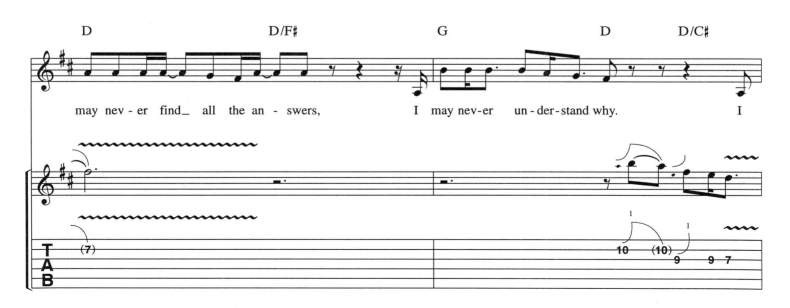

may nev-er find_ all the an-swers, I may nev-er un-der-stand why. I

142

may nev-er prove_ what I know to be true,_ but I know that I still have to try.__

If I___ die to-mor-row, I'd be all right be-cause_ I be-lieve_ that af-ter we're

Elec. Gtr. 1 tacet

Elec. Gtr. 1

Elec. Gtr. 2

Elec. Gtr. 2 *hold throughout*
(Played through Leslie spkr. cabinet)

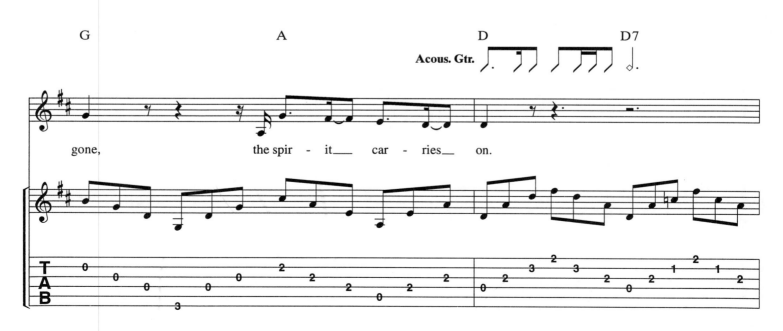

gone, the spir - it___ car - ries___ on.

Acous. Gtr.

*Hold bend and strike harmonic with right-hand index finger at fret 14.

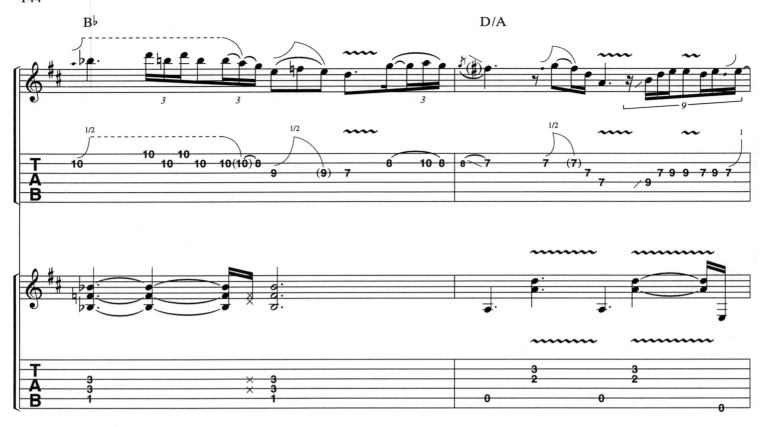

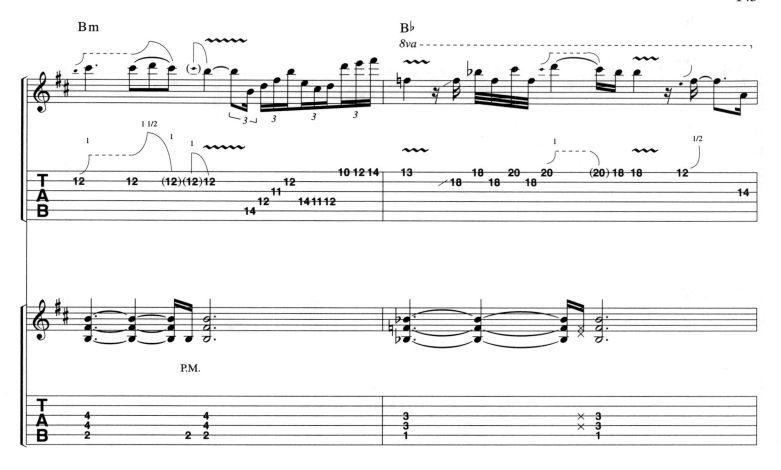

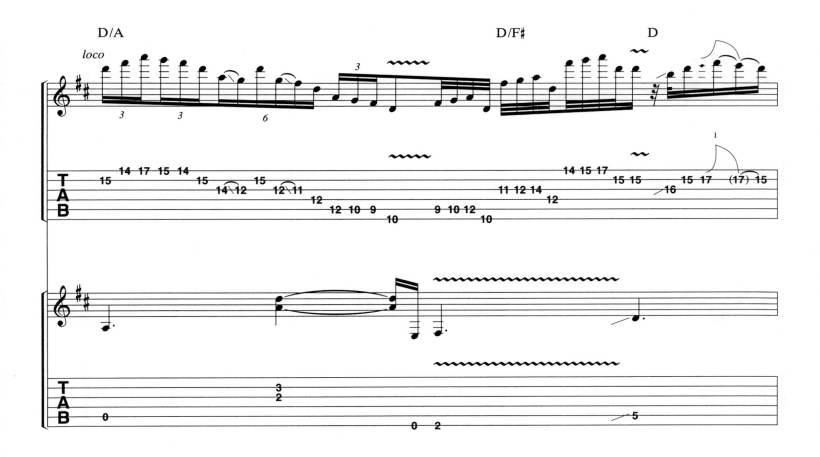

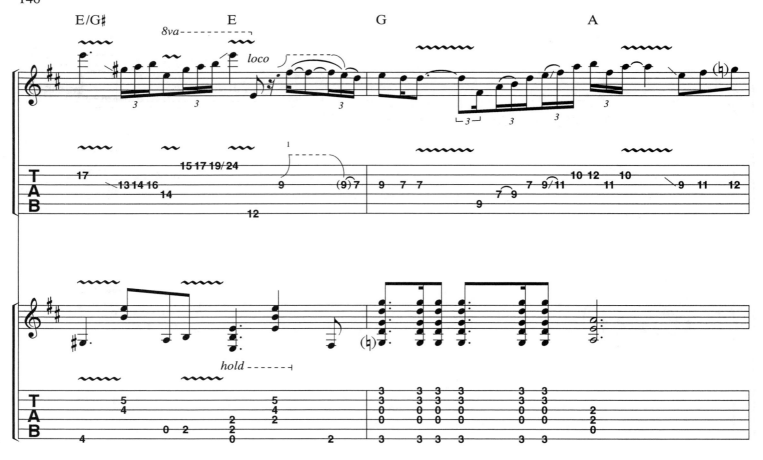

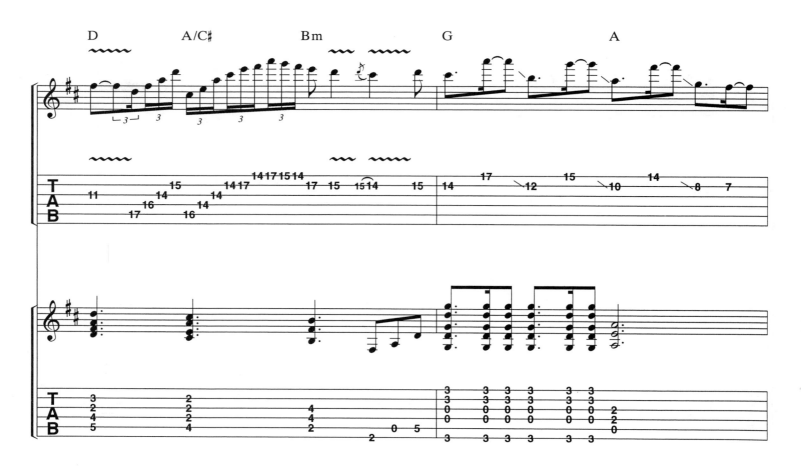

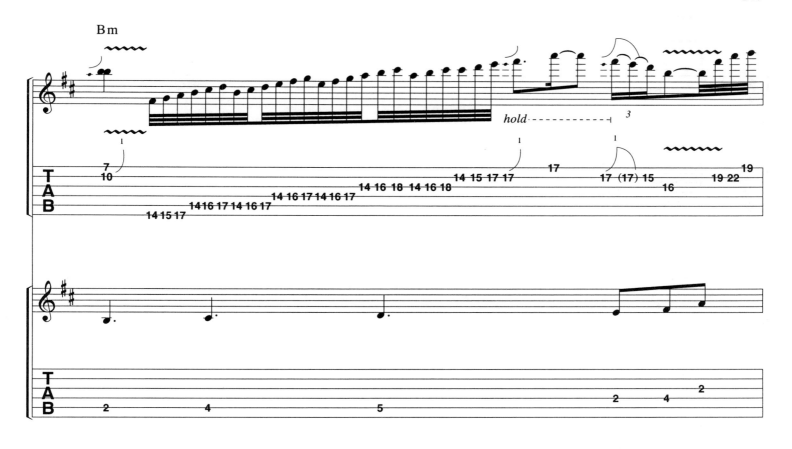

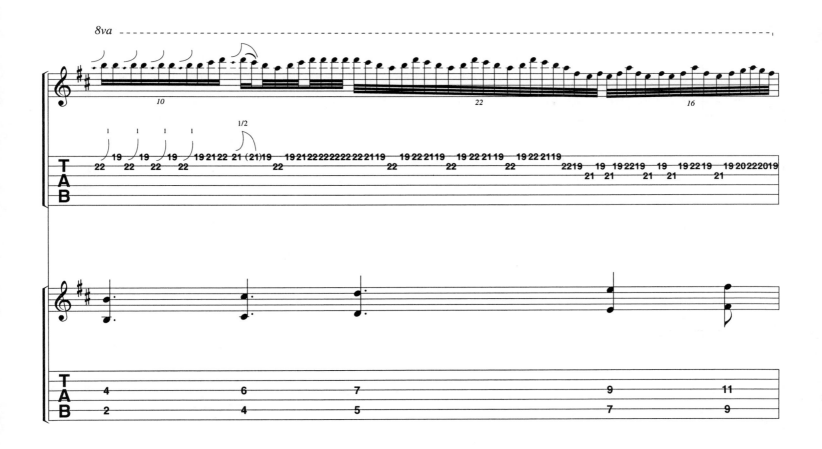

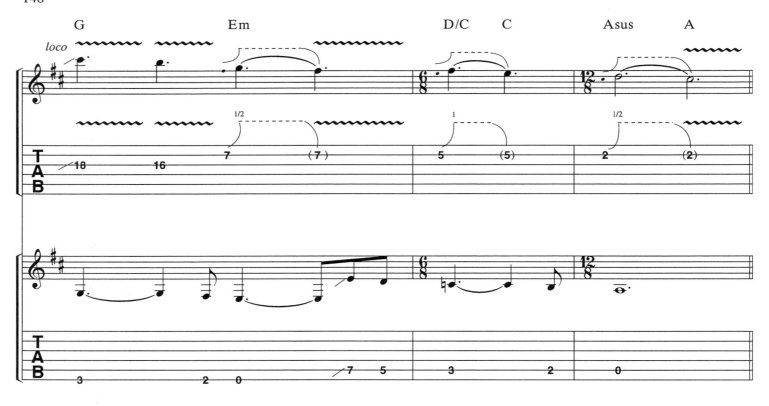

Verse 3:

Acous. Gtr. resume verse fig. simile

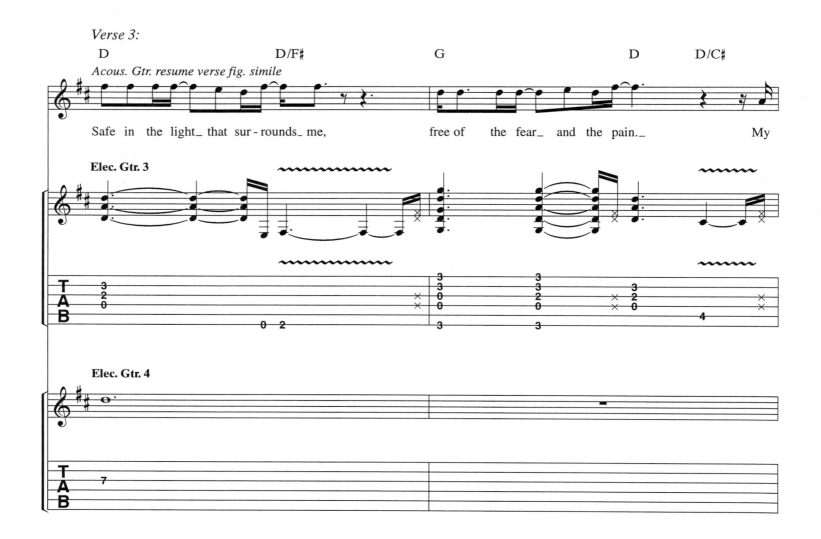

Safe in the light_ that sur - rounds_ me, free of the fear_ and the pain._ My

Elec. Gtr. 3

Elec. Gtr. 4

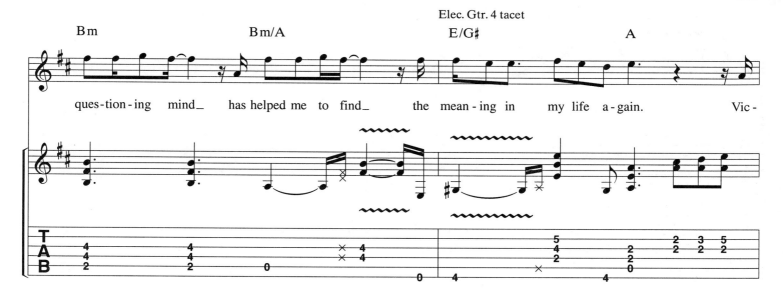

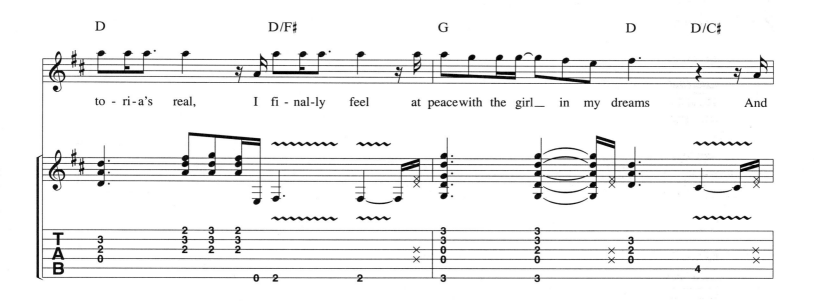

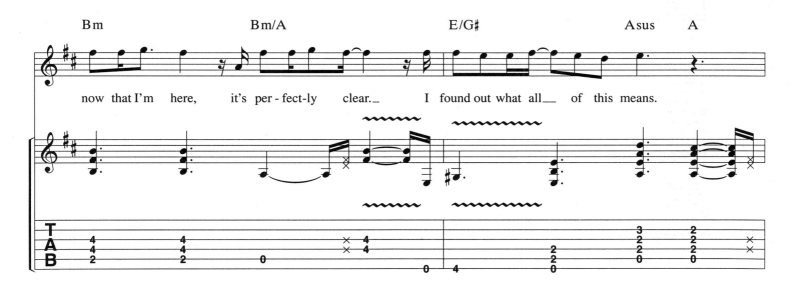

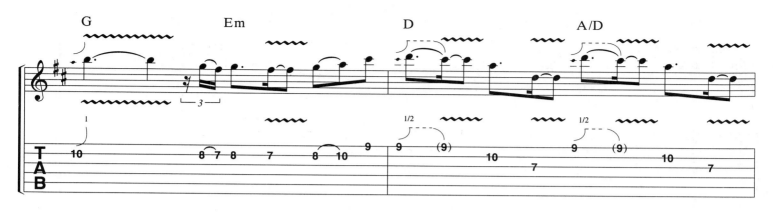

Scene Eight: The Spirit Carries On - 13 - 13
0441B

SCENE NINE: FINALLY FREE

Music by DREAM THEATER
Lyrics by MIKE PORTNOY

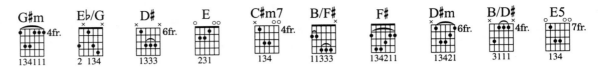

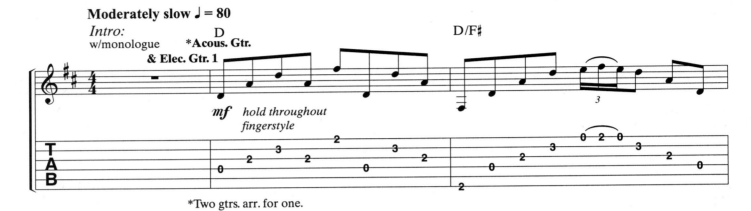

*Two gtrs. arr. for one.

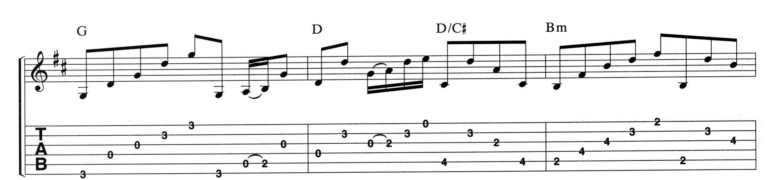

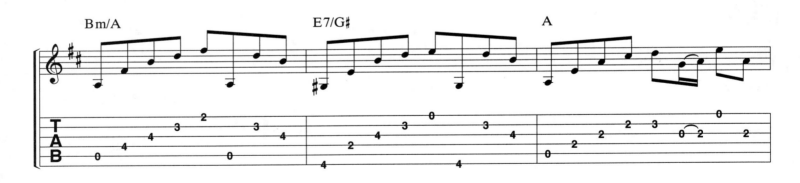

Scene Nine: Finally Free - 19 - 1
0441B

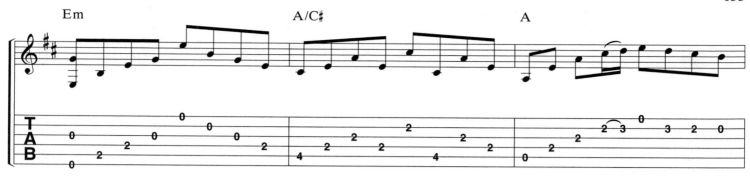

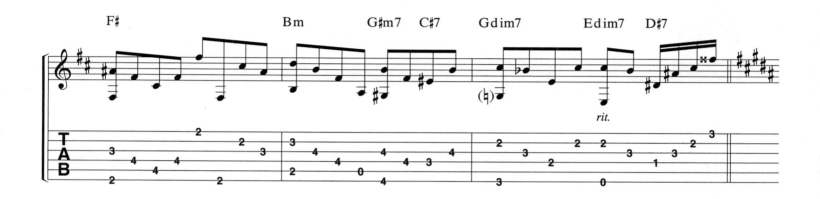

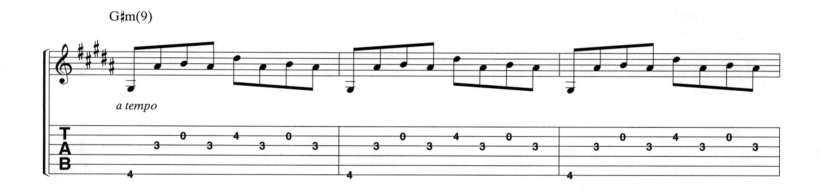

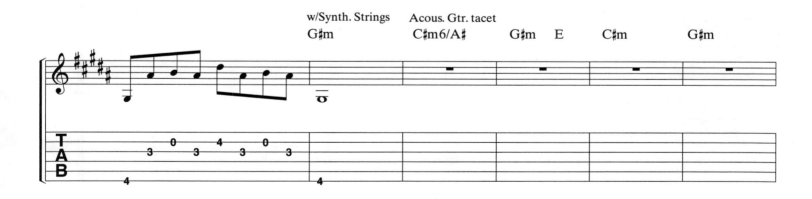

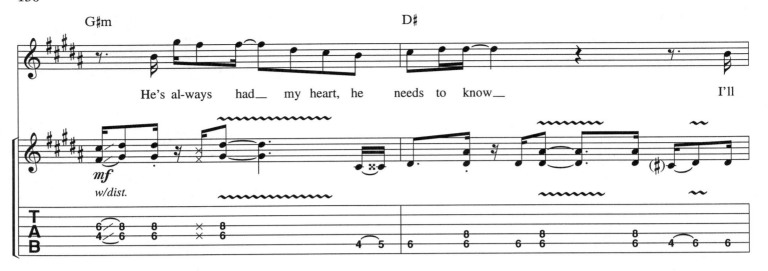

He's al-ways had__ my heart, he needs to know__   I'll

Chorus:
w/Rhy. Fig. 1 *(Acous. Gtr.)*
Elec. Gtr. 2 tacet

break free of the mir - a - cle;   it's time for him__ to go.__   This feel - ing

in - side__ me,   fi - n'lly found my love, I've   fi - n'lly broke__ free.

Bridge 1:
Acous. Gtr. tacet

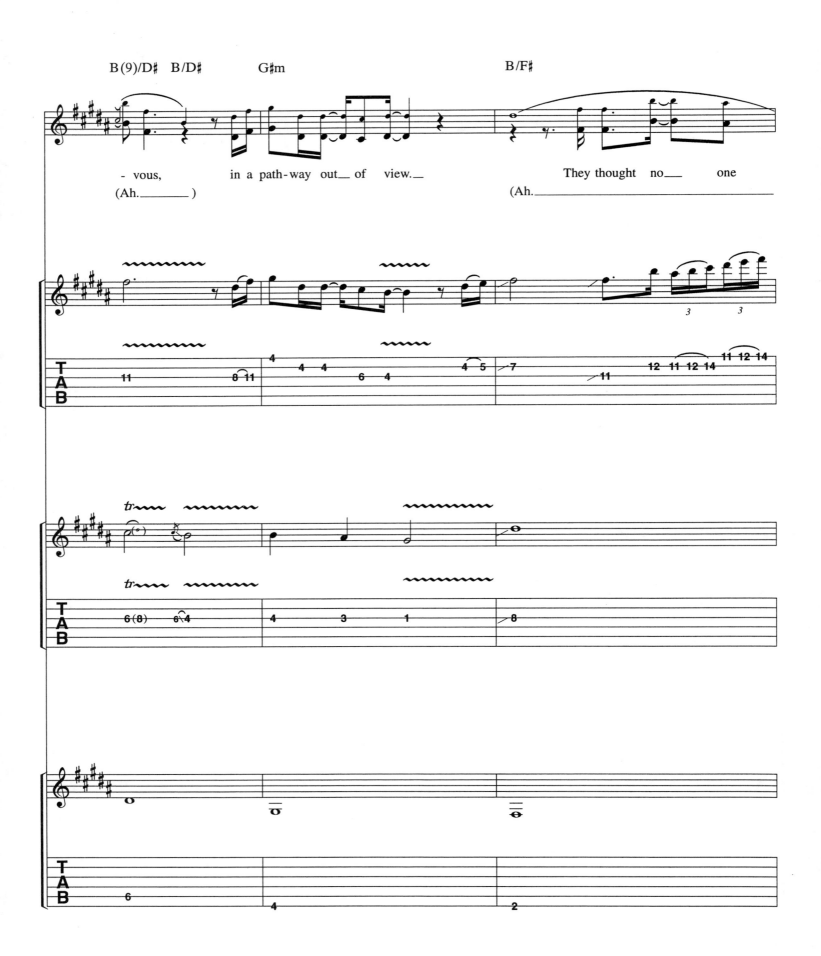

160

Scene Nine: Finally Free - 19 - 9
0441B

163

Bridge 3:

all their fears dis-ap-pear,_ it all be-comes_____ clear._____ A blind-ing light comes in - to

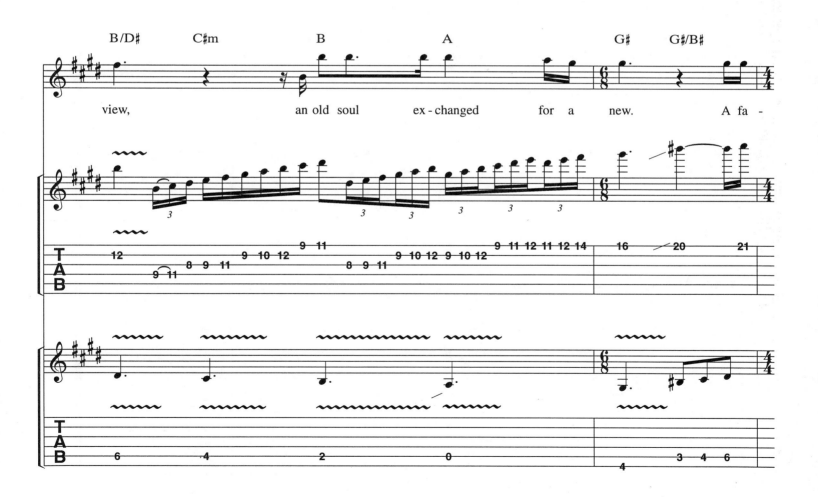

view, an old soul ex - changed for a new. A fa -

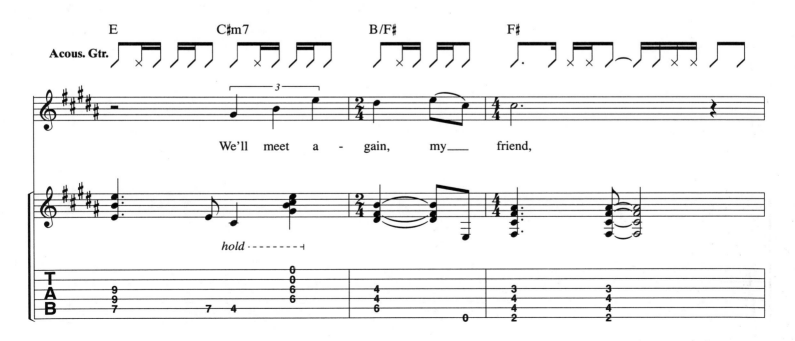

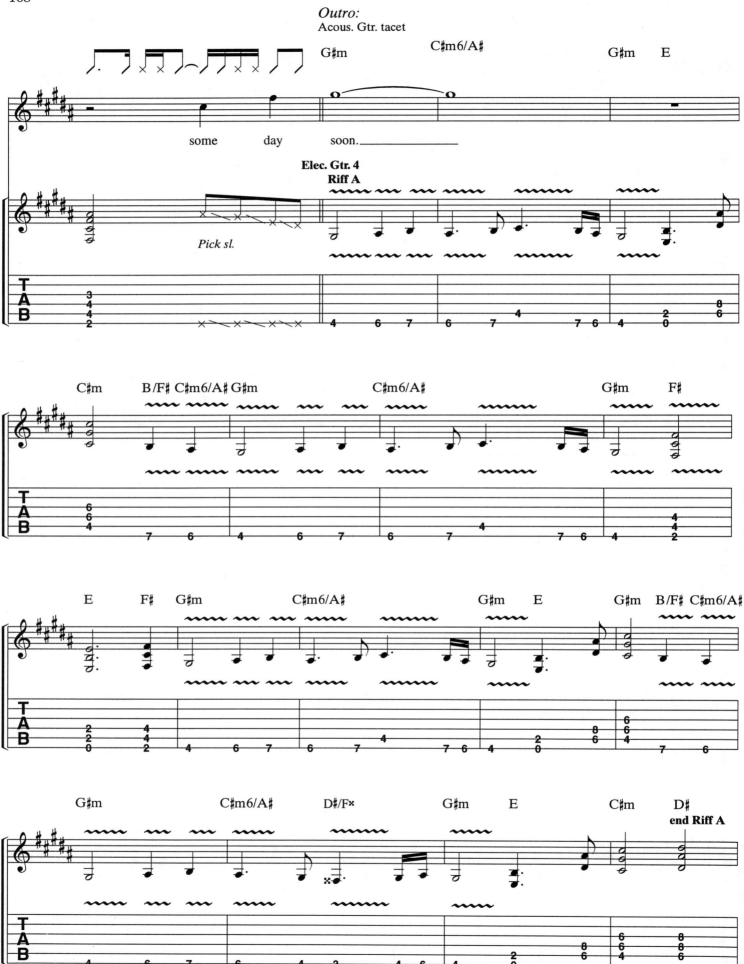

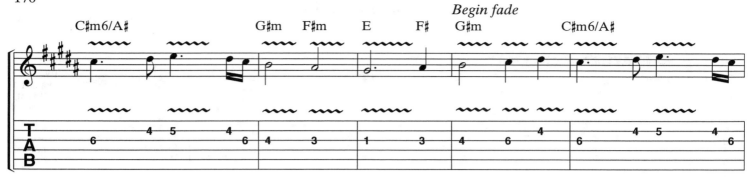

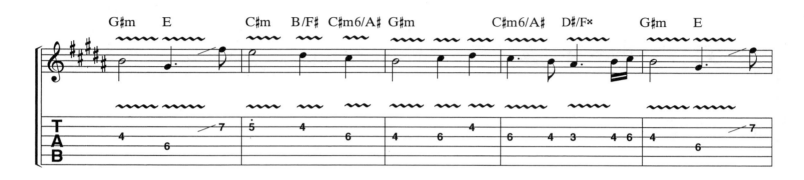

GUITAR TAB GLOSSARY **

TABLATURE EXPLANATION

READING TABLATURE: Tablature illustrates the six strings of the guitar. Notes and chords are indicated by the placement of fret numbers on a given string(s).

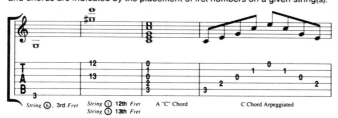

String ⑥, 3rd Fret   String ① 12th Fret   A "C" Chord   C Chord Arpeggiated
String ① 13th Fret

BENDING NOTES

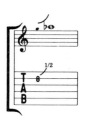

HALF STEP: Play the note and bend string one half step.*

WHOLE STEP: Play the note and bend string one whole step.

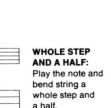

WHOLE STEP AND A HALF: Play the note and bend string a whole step and a half.

SLIGHT BEND (Microtone): Play the note and bend string slightly to the equivalent of half a fret.

PREBEND (Ghost Bend): Bend to the specified note, before the string is picked.

PREBEND AND RELEASE: Bend the string, play it, then release to the original note.

REVERSE BEND: Play the already-bent string, then immediately drop it down to the fretted note.

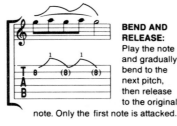

BEND AND RELEASE: Play the note and gradually bend to the next pitch, then release to the original note. Only the first note is attacked.

*A half step is the smallest interval in Western music; it is equal to one fret. A whole step equals two frets.

UNISON BEND: Play both notes and immediately bend the lower note to the same pitch as the higher note.

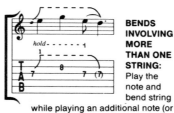

DOUBLE NOTE BEND: Play both notes and immediately bend both strings simultaneously.

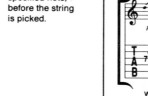

BENDS INVOLVING MORE THAN ONE STRING: Play the note and bend string while playing an additional note (or notes) on another string(s). Upon release, relieve pressure from additional note(s), causing original note to sound alone.

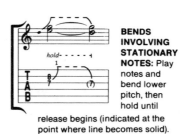

BENDS INVOLVING STATIONARY NOTES: Play notes and bend lower pitch, then hold until release begins (indicated at the point where line becomes solid).

TREMOLO BAR

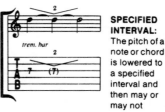

SPECIFIED INTERVAL: The pitch of a note or chord is lowered to a specified interval and then may or may not return to the original pitch. The activity of the tremolo bar is graphically represented by peaks and valleys.

UN-SPECIFIED INTERVAL: The pitch of a note or a chord is lowered to an unspecified interval.

HARMONICS

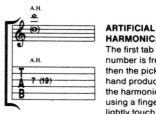

NATURAL HARMONIC: A finger of the fret hand lightly touches the note or notes indicated in the tab and is played by the pick hand.

ARTIFICIAL HARMONIC: The first tab number is fretted, then the pick hand produces the harmonic by using a finger to lightly touch the same string at the second tab number (in parenthesis) and is then picked by another finger.

ARTIFICIAL "PINCH" HAR-MONIC: A note is fretted as indicated by the tab, then the pick hand produces the harmonic by squeezing the pick firmly while using the tip of the index finger in the pick attack. If parenthesis are found around the fretted note, it does not sound. No parenthesis means both the fretted note and A.H. are heard simultaneously.

© 1990 Beam Me Up Music
c/o CPP/Belwin, Inc. Miami, Florida 33014
International Copyright Secured   Made in U.S.A.   All Rights Reserved

**By Kenn Chipkin and Aaron Stang

RHYTHM SLASHES

STRUM INDICA-TIONS: Strum with indicated rhythm. The chord voicings are found on the first page of the transcription underneath the song title.

INDICATING SINGLE NOTES USING RHYTHM SLASHES: Very often single notes are incorporated into a rhythm part. The note name is indicated above the rhythm slash with a fret number and a string indication.

ARTICULATIONS

HAMMER ON: Play lower note, then "hammer on" to higher note with another finger. Only the first note is attacked.

LEFT HAND HAMMER: Hammer on the first note played on each string with the left hand.

PULL OFF: Play higher note, then "pull off" to lower note with another finger. Only the first note is attacked.

FRET-BOARD TAPPING: "Tap" onto the note indicated by + with a finger of the pick hand, then pull off to the following note held by the fret hand.

TAP SLIDE: Same as fretboard tapping, but the tapped note is slid randomly up the fretboard, then pulled off to the following note.

BEND AND TAP TECHNIQUE: Play note and bend to specified interval. While holding bend, tap onto note indicated.

LEGATO SLIDE: Play note and slide to the following note. (Only first note is attacked).

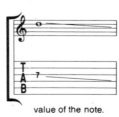

LONG GLISSAN-DO: Play note and slide in specified direction for the full value of the note.

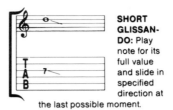

SHORT GLISSAN-DO: Play note for its full value and slide in specified direction at the last possible moment.

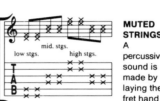

PICK SLIDE: Slide the edge of the pick in specified direction across the length of the string(s).

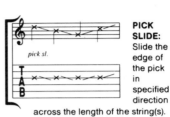

MUTED STRINGS: A percussive sound is made by laying the fret hand across all six strings while pick hand strikes specified area (low, mid, high strings).

PALM MUTE: The note or notes are muted by the palm of the pick hand by lightly touching the string(s) near the bridge.

TREMOLO PICKING: The note or notes are picked as fast as possible.

TRILL: Hammer on and pull off consecutively and as fast as possible between the original note and the grace note.

ACCENT: Notes or chords are to be played with added emphasis.

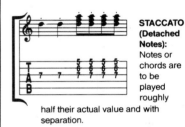

STACCATO (Detached Notes): Notes or chords are to be played roughly half their actual value and with separation.

DOWN STROKES AND UPSTROKES: Notes or chords are to be played with either a downstroke (⊓) or upstroke (∨) of the pick.

VIBRATO: The pitch of a note is varied by a rapid shaking of the fret hand finger, wrist, and forearm.